4 POWER LEADERSHIP®

YOUR PATHWAY TO LEADERSHIP SUCCESS

Daniel A. Shyti

4 POWER ENTERPRISES

4 Power Enterprises, LLC
POTOMAC FALLS, VIRGINIA

4 Power Enterprises, LLC
P.O. Box 651132
Potomac Falls, VA 20165
www.4PowerLeadership.com
Inquiry@4PowerLeadership.com

Book Layout ©2013 BookDesignTemplates.com

Ordering information for quantity sales:
Special discounts are available on quantity purchases by corporations, associations, and others. For details, contact the "Special Sales Department" at the address above.

4 Power Leadership/ Daniel A. Shyti. —1st ed.
ISBN 978-0-9897084-2-5

PRAISE FOR *4 POWER LEADERSHIP*

"I personally benefited from Dan's coaching and advice – quiet, insightful, never heavy-handed, it always made me reflect for hours and days after it was delivered."

— *Albert Lulushi, Technology Executive, Author, and Entrepreneur*

"Dan is an inspirational leader who mentored me as a friend and colleague in the Business Development organization. He was always willing to take on new challenges and to champion organizational change for the betterment of our team."

— *Patricia Sego, Capture Manager, Computer Sciences Corporation*

"Dan is a masterful strategist and speaker. It seems there is nothing Dan cannot do when he sets his mind to it!"

— *Talisa Ernstmann, President, Ernstmann Consulting*

"Dan is a keen observer of human behavior and knows how to inspire people to achieve their best results. As Dan points out, leadership is not merely a characteristic of a chosen few. It is an ongoing process of hard work, introspection and focus. "

— *Tricia Branagan, Sr. Marketing Specialist, L-3 Communications*

"While working on my master's degree one of my assignments was to identify the traits and characteristics of a leader we aspired to be more like. That task was a 'no-brainer', from learning about his personal life to experiencing his professional prowess; I can honestly say Mr. Dan Shyti is the best. Thank you Dan!"

— *Bryan Powers, Sr. Systems engineer*

"Dan possesses great insight and has the boldness to tell it like it is."

— Frank McGoldrick, Program Manager, L-3 Communications

"Dan Shyti is a natural leader who willingly shares his leadership experience."

— Lee Cooper, President, Cooper Growth Strategies, LLC

"Dan is a consummate professional and executive. He is a man of ethics and high quality professional skills. Dan is a leader, visionary and innovator who always delivers value."

— John Guenther, Sr. Account Executive

Contents

In loving memory of my parents,
Todi and Gina Shyti.
Their life story is a constant source of inspiration to me.

Preface

L eadership is the foundational skill through which any communal goal is accomplished. Any goal that requires coordinated action by a team also requires someone to visualize the end result, organize the team, and provide the sustaining inspiration to see the task through to attainment of the goal. The essence of leadership is simple, but mastering the art takes commitment.

4 Power Leadership is a simple roadmap for learning the art of leadership based on a philosophy of self-awareness and personal growth. Whether you are just starting on the path of leadership or have been in a leadership position for some time, *4 Power Leadership* will inspire you to expand your skills to the next level.

I've encountered some great leaders during the course of my career. However, I have also repeatedly encountered a shortage of effective leadership in companies I worked for as well as in the Army. There are several reasons for this shortage: insufficient training, weakness in corporate culture, and lack of mentorship. This book provides guidance and advice on effective leadership techniques, presents methods for strengthening corporate culture, and identifies ways to help close the mentorship gap.

In the early part of my career, I spent a great deal of time learning to lead by trial and error. That's a difficult and time-consuming method for learning anything, especially something as challenging as leadership. I discovered that I was not alone in my struggle to master leadership in the corporate environment. Here's a common scenario I've encountered repeatedly:

"Congratulations! We're promoting you to supervisor. You've worked hard and earned the promotion. Take charge of your department and make it work. Have a nice day."

This is how first-line leadership positions are filled on a routine basis. Sadly, too many competent or standout performers are suddenly thrust into leadership positions without any training. It is exactly how I landed in my first post-military leadership position.

Fortunately, I was able to succeed in my first assignment as a project leader. However, with no leadership training, many newly-appointed managers quickly begin to make serious mistakes in handling personnel assigned to their teams. Before long, sniping, dysfunction, resignations, and defections become the behavioral norm. The organization begins to unravel from the bottom up. The frontline organization starts failing to meet the needs of its internal and external customers. Pressure builds. By the time senior management becomes aware or has time to react to the problem, dysfunction has spread upward and across the organization. These circumstances often lead to a crisis, and the organization's time is then consumed with putting out the fire instead of focusing on elevating its performance.

An even more insidious outcome is when the crisis doesn't occur, and the organization's deteriorating performance is not immediately obvious to leaders at the top. Sometimes the organization suffering from poor leadership in the middle and lower ranks simply erodes into a semi-functioning state where low performance is the accepted norm. This condition saps the strength, enthusiasm, and morale of an organization.

Later on, the untrained first-line leader may job hop to another company and be promoted to the next management level. Sometimes the untrained manager is promoted all the way up to the executive ranks without ever having had any formal leadership training. More tragically, junior managers, not knowing any better, begin to emulate the ineffective behavior of the executives who never had any training thinking the approach they see is effective leadership. The cycle of ineffective leadership is then perpetually reinforced. My frustration with this condition is the inspiration for *4 Power Leadership.*

How can we possibly expect to create the dynamic and bold senior leaders of tomorrow if they routinely begin their leadership career without any point of reference? My first reason for writing this book is to provide that link to effective leadership that will help you improve your skills, whether you're currently in a leadership position or aspiring to obtain one.

My second reason for writing this book is to emphasize that organizational cultures must shift to emphasize the pursuit of individual virtue as a core leadership quality. Virtue extends way beyond simple honesty. Virtues are the set of qualities that define one's character. Character is integral to leadership. Leadership drives performance. Leadership rooted in virtue is the soundest method for producing a strengthened and more positive corporate culture that will transfer results to the bottom line. More importantly, a commitment to virtue-based leadership can avoid severe leadership failures that lead to disasters and scandal.

Our current collective approach toward growing future leaders is practically tragic. As I've already noted, we appoint far too many people to leadership positions with little or no training. Then, we don't make virtue the center of leadership culture. Further, we compound both of these problems by not providing sufficient mentorship for our emerging leaders.

New leaders are in an especially difficult situation. Not only are they entering their first assignments without a proper frame of reference, but they also lack access to worthy role models. Even when effective role models exist within corporations and other organizations, mentorship is often not available to junior leaders. Who can new leaders look to as mentors and role models? Where can they find real mentorship? How can emerging leaders overcome the mentorship vacuum?

This brings me to the third reason for writing *4 Power Leadership*. This book will help fill the mentorship vacuum by providing valuable and focused insight into the personal powers you must possess to be effective in any leadership position. I will also suggest ways you can find the mentorship you need.

This book is written from the perspective of corporate life, but the techniques and ideas are readily adaptable to any circumstance involving leadership. It is intended to not only serve as a clear how-to manual, but also as a roadmap for development of the leadership skills you will need throughout your career. The book will also identify tested sources for leadership learning that I've turned to over the course of my career.

Who should read *4 Power Leadership?* Anyone who:

- Is an established professional or is new to leadership
- Is already in a leadership position and wants to improve effectiveness
- Is a CEO or corporate executive who has inherited a mess and needs to rebuild the corporate culture
- Is interested in knowing what constitutes effective leadership.

The majority of problems we face in society are largely self-inflicted due to poor leadership both in government and the corporate world, but our choices are simple. We can sit idly on the sidelines as spectators, or we can do something about it. *4 Power Leadership* is my attempt to do something about it. My goal is to ignite the discussion of virtue as the centerpiece of leadership training for all types of organizations. My desire is to inspire good people, who don't necessarily see themselves as leaders now, to rise up and enter the ranks of leadership. If they do, this will enlarge the pool of virtuous people who are qualified and available to lead. Even if you never assume a position of leadership, knowledge of what makes a good leader is essential in knowing who to follow.

As you read, keep the following thoughts in the forefront of your mind: When we are seeking answers, life hides a lesson for us under every rock. Lessons sometimes come to us from unlikely sources. Just about every person and every situation can teach us something we can file away for future use. It is important to always capture the good from a source of learning and throw away the bad. This book references numerous extraordinary historic people who have distinguished themselves as exceptional leaders. Some of the historic figures I refer to may be controversial to some readers. You don't have to support all of their actions, but again you can accept the good and throw away the bad. Continually look for individuals with effective leadership traits who produce results. Study both their successes and failures. Pay particular attention to how they react to failures and turn things around toward success.

You should also pay attention to the context of a leader's decisions. Specific leadership decisions are closely tied to the times and circumstances in which they occur. We must judge the great leaders of the past within this context, not the present. Learning from a multitude of past situations, people, and experiences is a powerful way to enhance personal leadership ability.

Many of the stories, techniques, and situations discussed in this book are derived from my life experience, observations, and the resources I have tapped to improve my own leadership skills. When I use examples from my personal life or stories contributed from others, I either don't mention a name or may substitute a fictitious name if the example casts someone in a less than positive light. The exception to this rule is public information about public figures. It's not my intent to denigrate others, but rather to provide valuable examples for learning.

Finally, I'm a simple guy, and I like to get straight to the heart of any issue, understand it, and organize it in a way that's easy to communicate. As the great artist and inventor Leonardo da Vinci once said:

"Simplicity is the ultimate sophistication."

Learning leadership excellence requires a simple model that demystifies the process of becoming a leader. *4 Power Leadership* is that simple model by which a leader can consistently gauge his or her own personal effectiveness.

Dan Shyti
Potomac Falls, Virginia
July 2013

Acknowledgements

First and foremost, a big thank you to my wife, Jackie, for her love and support and the faith she has placed in me to embark on this great journey.

Thank you to my children, Nicole and Danny, who are not only my pride and joy, but have also contributed their time and talent to making *4 Power Leadership* a quality product.

Many, many thanks to my dear friend, Stan Young, whose amazing editorial comments helped keep the direction of this book on track. You are a great human being.

Thank you to Kathleen Ferris, *The HR Whisperer*, who provided some outstanding comments and helped validate some of the book's perspectives.

Thank you to long-time friend Lee Begeja for your commentary and discussion. You're a terrific person with a sharp mind.

Thank you to Lee Cooper, friend and mentor, who gave generously of his time in serving as a sounding board for ideas.

An Introduction to Leadership

CHAPTER 1

Is Leadership for You?

"If your actions inspire others to dream more, learn more, do more, and become more, you are a leader."

– *John Quincy Adams*

L eadership is the ability to mobilize people toward a common goal. It comes with a great deal of responsibility that increases with the size and scope of the organization in the leader's charge. Effective leadership is a personal quality that is in high demand around the world. In difficult times, the demand for effective leadership only intensifies. People from every walk of life and at every level of an organization look for leadership. They expect it, need it, and deserve it.

Leadership is a calling and a way of life. If you have a burning desire to inspire others to strive for greatness and become more than they think they can be, then I strongly encourage you to step forward and assume the mantle of leadership.

Leadership can bring many rewards. As a leader, the personal satisfaction of achieving a goal with a well-organized team is indeed profound. Collectively, everyone's spirits reach a new level of inspiration. There's something special about harmonious collaboration and knowing that a united team effort succeeded in achieving a goal. As the leader who orchestrated the effort, you experience a deep sense of satisfaction as you watch your team celebrate its success.

Leadership will bring out the best in you if you commit to upholding virtues. When you are leading and you know that other people are looking to you as the pacesetter, you must always remain on the moral high ground and be an example for others through your actions. Failing to stay on the moral high ground will instantly undermine your authority to lead. Leadership will challenge you to be the best person you can be.

Leadership will reward you with personal fulfillment through the realization of your ideas. As the leader, the objectives you set are the ones that will be achieved. Through leadership, you will have the capability to shape your corner of the world. You will see the achievements around you as a reflection of your work. It is deeply rewarding when your vision is realized.

It is said that leadership has its privileges. Financial rewards often accompany leadership. Once you master the techniques of leadership and develop a track record of delivering results, you will become a valuable asset. Organizations will seek you out to take on important projects or endeavors. Ironically though, the most admired and successful leaders weren't driven by monetary rewards – they were driven by a desire for achievement and service to others. They became excellent leaders and the financial rewards invariably followed.

On the other hand, leadership is not a role that should be accepted lightly. As a leader, you must realize that your subordinates and others will be examining your every word and every move. It is a role that carries constant pressure and demands. You will be looked upon for direction, reassurance, and inspiration even when you're not feeling particularly inspired yourself. In leadership, you will not only attract admiration and support, but you will also become a magnet for criticism, jealousy, and subversion. By sharpening your leadership abilities, you must prepare to achieve your goals while absorbing criticisms that will inevitably be directed at you.

If you are considering leadership solely for personal gain, I encourage you to reassess your motives. Those who are in it for the money or other selfish reasons fall into the pile of negative leaders. This group typically achieves short-term success, but ultimately their selfish perspective undermines their temporary gain.

Negative Leaders

Generally, people in positions of authority are called "leaders." However, when you examine their qualities and behaviors, you will see that only a small percentage of them meet the criteria of true leaders. In fact, many people who hold power are too often negative leaders.

Negative leaders can easily be identified through a common set of characteristics. People follow a negative leader because they have no choice. Failure to follow the leader's directives will be met with punitive actions. This creates a culture of constant fear and intimidation that permeates throughout the entire organization. In fact, subordinate leaders in this type of organization are often more ruthless than the negative leader at the top because they feel they have carte blanche to act as they please as long as their actions are aligned with their superior.

The negative leader has a deficit of virtue and a bankrupt moral code. He will lie, cheat, steal, bully, and do whatever he can get away with as long as he gets his way. The negative leader subscribes to rules that will work for the moment. He disregards consideration of the greatest good for the greatest number for the greatest duration.

The negative leader creates enemies easily. With such aggressive and forceful tactics as his modus operandi, the negative leader consistently sows resentment and fear. Ironically, the fear that he uses to control adversaries will also drive his followers to act against him when they become fearful that they will soon become targets. Ultimately, the negative leader is doomed to failure and disgrace. With his list of enemies growing, it's only a matter of time before someone takes him down. In the usually non-lethal corporate world, it will be through dismissal. In the political world, the negative leader will be taken down through the disgrace of a lost election (if he's lucky to live in a democracy) or through violence, as is often the case in dictatorships.

Positive Leaders

In contrast, the positive leader inspires people to be better. Their spirits are lifted in his presence. As a result, people willingly follow his direction because they see it as the right thing to do.

The positive leader serves as a role model to his subordinates. The people who follow him yearn to be like him because they see the higher calling of the principles by which he is guided. They know that he can be counted on to do the "right thing" above all else. The environment he creates and promotes is a positive, principle-based environment where virtues are guideposts.

Leaders Are Made

Though you may feel the pull of leadership as a career path, you may doubt that you have what it takes. After all, aren't leaders somehow born to lead? Take heart; leadership can most definitely be learned. Vince Lombardi, the legendary football coach of the Green Bay Packers said it best:

"Leaders aren't born; they are made. And they are made just like anything else, through hard work. And that's the price we'll have to pay to achieve that goal, or any goal."

Are you ready to put in the hard work necessary to sharpen your leadership ability? It will take discipline and patience as you work on developing the required skills and techniques.

Years ago, I heard a speaker make the comment, "You can't teach leadership. You learn it." I later discovered that this was also a piece of "Lombardian" wisdom. At first, I was confused by the quote. After all, how can you learn something that can't be taught? The answer is simple. You could identify all the qualities and principles a leader must live by and regurgitate every one of those principles in the exact order in which they were presented. Still, you would not be a leader. To become an effective leader, the essential qualities and principles must become ingrained in your personality. Leadership must become a way of life for you. It takes more than simple training. Becoming a great leader requires a maturation of your spirit by adopting the pursuit of virtue as a way of life in addition to honing the specific skills required of leaders. This can only be achieved through deep commitment and consistent action.

My hope is that *4 Power Leadership* will be the catalyst that propels you on your path to becoming a more effective leader.

---

4 Power Thoughts

1. Do you feel drawn to positions of leadership? Why or why not?
2. Have you ever suffered from the effects of poor leadership?
3. Have you been taught that leaders are born?
   a. Do you believe that?

CHAPTER 2

Where Have All the Good Leaders Gone?

"Our chief want is someone who will inspire us to be what we know we could be."

– *Ralph Waldo Emerson*

L eadership development is important not just for reasons of good corporate citizenship and good societal values, but because it makes good business sense as well. Growth is constrained by the number of available effective leaders from which an organization can draw. In formative stages, organizations usually place a great deal of importance on the first few strategic hires for key leadership positions. As an organization becomes successful and starts to grow, the number of qualified leaders available to fuel further growth must be sustained in order for any organization to scale properly. If the growth of quality leaders is not sustained, a leadership vacuum develops between the few competent leaders at the top and the employees on the front lines. With weak leadership in the middle, it becomes very difficult for senior leaders to transmit their influence and continue to execute corporate plans.

Earlier in this book, I said that leadership structure is undermined by poor leadership development and weaknesses in corporate culture. In this chapter, you'll learn more about the reasons organizations do not grow their leaders effectively.

Poor leadership training – Depending on the size of the company and resources available, there may not be any formal training provided to employees who are assigned leadership responsibility. The training programs that do exist are unlikely to focus on the nuances of interpersonal interaction, which is the central skill of leadership. In addition, the training probably doesn't encourage individuals to gain self-knowledge as a first step in becoming a leader. In my experience, when leadership programs are provided, there is very little emphasis on a formal program of introspection. It is this self-examination that is necessary to produce a well-balanced and mature leader. How can leaders interact effectively with others if they have not balanced themselves internally first?

Inadequate mentorship – Productive mentorship is very hard to establish. There are several obstacles that must be overcome, not the least of which is availability of the mentor's time. Usually, the most effective leaders are also the people with the busiest schedules. Setting aside precious time on their calendars can prove difficult.

While it's true that some people are genuinely altruistic and want to "mentor" someone, generally that's not the case. In today's corporate arena, managers are already overscheduled and pressed for time. Given their responsibilities to their employer as well as their own personal obligations, it's not surprising that people hesitate in becoming a mentor. After all, in blunt terms, what's the return on investment for a mentor? What does the mentor get in return for openly sharing his or her secrets and lifetime experiences? Selfless giving isn't necessarily a sufficient enticement for a leader to engage in mentorship. Although occasionally a leader wants to pass knowledge on to the next generation as part of his legacy, this type of altruism is almost always reserved for close personal friends or family. Mentees often exacerbate this problem because they look at mentors simply as a means to get ahead instead of taking a genuine interest in learning from the mentor's life experience. There has to be a good reason to establish a mentoring relationship. A smart mentee will show genuine interest in the mentor as a catalyst for the relationship.

The mentor may also have concerns about crossing the line of professional distance. The mentor and mentee will get to know one another quite well. This conflicts with the traditional notion that a leader must maintain an adequate distance from subordinates. The mentor must feel absolutely comfortable in establishing the relationship required to provide true mentoring for leadership training. The mentee can help ease this concern by maintaining professional respect for the mentor.

Discomfort with close personal relationships is another obstacle in mentoring. Many leaders who have great presence in front of a crowd may be uncomfortable in intimate one-on-one settings. Perhaps, the individual has learned to be guarded as a way to counter vulnerability. Sometimes the leader just doesn't excel in close personal relationships. In this case, a mentoring relationship can actually provide personal growth for the mentor as well by exercising his interpersonal skills.

Of all the obstacles to establishing functional and productive mentorships, selfishness is probably the most self-defeating of all. Many leaders can't help but feel insecure at the top. Just as they may have established an adoring following, they've probably made some enemies along the way as well. They tend to look over their shoulders fearing that someone is vying for their job or trying to discredit them. After an agonizing climb to the top, the last thing some leaders want is other strong leaders around them who can challenge them for supremacy. You would think that leaders would want to extend their influence to the maximum by surrounding themselves with a team of the strongest possible leaders. Leaders may say they want to strengthen organizational leadership, but few are truly comfortable with other strong leaders around them.

Some leaders tend to surround themselves with fawning staff ready to jump at every request and unlikely to challenge or question the leader's guidance. This situation can be a reflection of a weakness in the leader's character such as an overinflated ego or personal insecurity. Unbridled resistance to leadership direction is clearly an unacceptable condition, but mindless compliance is every bit as detrimental. If ideas are never tested and challenged, then an organization is unlikely to innovate from within through creative alternatives or new ideas.

Inadequate empowerment – Lack of empowerment is another significant factor that inhibits leader development and contributes to the leadership vacuum. Generally, senior leaders simply do not sufficiently empower leaders below them. In this type of environment, subordinates are not capable of completing anything independently. The senior leader who restricts empowerment creates a central bottleneck through one single person or a small group of persons, thereby slowing organizational productivity and nimbleness to a crawl. Because of this bottleneck in the organization, the supervisor who now has to make all the decisions typically cannot keep up with the pace and demand for decision making. This results in last minute executive interjection caused by previously unaddressed issues that should have been handled much earlier in the process. As junior leaders become more accustomed to punting decisions up to the next rung on the corporate ladder, they exercise their leadership skills less and less. In effect, their skills atrophy and they become paper shufflers instead of leaders.

Many C-level executives have commented that lack of empowerment is on the rise in both corporations and government. This can be explained by several factors: complexity of the business environment due to the threat of litigation; regulation such as the Sarbanes-Oxley Act that has led to the perpetuation of bureaucracy inside large corporations and dilution of decision-making authority; overreaction to malfeasance and poor decisions causing authority to be pulled upward in the management chain; and ineffective senior leadership.

These days, everyone is afraid of lawsuits. The desire to avoid costly litigation and potential damage to one's career provides incentive for senior leaders to micromanage and over-check everything. Combining this fear with the demands of regulations leads to reduction in leader empowerment. I've seen organizations that have six layers of approvals for decisions that could easily be made at much lower levels. This is a crushing blow to nimbleness in a competitive business climate, and it's a deathblow to leader development because junior leaders never receive the opportunity to grow under the responsibility and authority that is created by empowerment. An even more damaging side effect is that micromanagement erodes trust throughout the organization and drags the culture down.

The regulatory contribution to reduction of empowerment is typically an overreaction to malfeasance and/or failure. As a result of criminal corporate behavior and malfeasance in recent years, there has been a knee-jerk reaction to create more rules to prevent reoccurrence. However, this seldom works to stop the next event. Criminals by definition operate outside the law. Nothing written on paper will ever stop them from doing as they please. However, the added burden of more rules and over-checking mostly affects people who are already doing the right thing and has a profound negative effect on corporate agility.

Furthermore, when someone in an organization makes a serious but honest mistake, a common reaction by the senior manager is to say, "From now on, I'll make those decisions." The implicit message is that no one below his or her level is smart enough or capable enough to bear certain responsibility. This is simply poor leadership strategy. The more effective response is to boost training and reemphasize performance standards.

All of these factors, among others, cause senior leaders to pull authority upward away from more junior leaders and thereby negatively impact the opportunity for leadership growth through experience.

I once worked for a small business as a senior project manager. As a small company, we couldn't afford all the overhead staff with intersecting interests that is commonly found in large companies. I therefore had a great deal of autonomy. I made important business decisions every day. I hired and fired people, authorized expenses, negotiated contract terms, and approved technical direction of the projects I managed. It was empowerment nirvana! Guess what happened? We completed our projects on time and within budget. Imagine that! Empowerment worked. Effective empowerment merely requires that leaders teach, coach, and establish an understanding of what is out of bounds. The trend toward destruction of empowerment must be reversed if an organization is to succeed. Bill George, former CEO and best-selling author, summarized this thought most succinctly:

"The key to leadership in the twenty-first century is to empower people."

The most capable aren't necessarily chosen as leaders – Another contributing factor to the leadership vacuum is that the best leaders don't always succeed in achieving positions of authority. It's a politically charged world out there. Sometimes the politics of advancement have absolutely nothing to do with being excellent. The less effective performers who play golf in the right power circles will beat out a dedicated person who does not make time for political interaction. A less effective performer but politically astute player can move ahead of the dedicated worker. It happens all too frequently.

In other cases, people who attain positions of authority sometimes gain this power through the exercise of deceit and treachery. Principled people who would make fine leaders may get shut out of leadership opportunities because they rightly are unwilling to play nasty political games that they view as compromising their ethics. To their detriment, they are also unaware of the treachery that surrounds them and fail to defend against it.

Leadership is difficult to teach – Leadership excellence requires a commitment to a way of life in addition to acquiring the right set of skills. There are certainly skills to be learned and mastered in leadership. However, the practice of leadership also requires that the very essence of an individual become transformed by internalizing the qualities, virtues, and ideals of leadership. Leadership is something you carry with you every day as part of who you are. The transformation to a leadership persona is dependent upon how quickly one can adopt good habits associated with positive leadership behavior while replacing bad habits. Of course, as with any endeavor, the more you immerse yourself in good habits, the more rapidly the transformation can occur. Be prepared to commitment to a lifelong learning process.

Management is not leadership – Teaching management in place of leadership can stifle leadership growth. Managers track processes. Leaders rally people to a common cause. Teaching management does not make someone a leader, yet this continues to be the main focus of most business schools and corporate training programs.

Self-limitation – Sometimes people place limitations on themselves without realizing it. This prevents otherwise capable people from attaining their true potential as leaders. Self-limitation is the one factor hindering leadership growth that is totally within an individual's power to change through personal determination.

My firsthand experience with this condition occurred while I was still in college. One day, a friend surprised me with an unexpected career plan. He had visited an Army recruiter and was planning to join the Reserve Officer Training Corps (ROTC). It was quite a shock since no one in our circle of friends was considering the military as a career path. My friend encouraged me to visit with the recruiter as well.

The recruiter told me about the ROTC program and the opportunities the Army could provide. He told me that I would be trained to be a leader. It was a light-bulb moment! No one had ever told me before that I could be transformed into a leader. The concept of being a leader began to intrigue me. That day was a turning point in my life. I began to see myself differently. My leadership transformation had begun.

I did eventually join ROTC and spent four years in the Army where I made lots of mistakes, but I also grew immensely as a leader thanks to the extraordinary responsibility that is placed on young officers. It was a rewarding experience that was created by the removal of an unconscious limitation I had placed on myself.

Lack of discipline – Reinforcing effective leadership practices within an organization takes serious discipline. Those you lead reflect everything you do back at you. Therefore, leaders at the top must always project the desired behavior and performance standards. If they procrastinate, procrastination will be perpetuated throughout the organization. If lack of attention to detail is evident in senior leaders, the organization will have quality issues. If leaders don't take deadlines seriously, then everything will be late. Failure to adhere to the high standards required of effective leadership can ripple downward in an organization. This can establish a negative leadership culture that will have severely damaging effects by setting low leadership standards for everyone.

Corporations should be very concerned with the limited availability of effective leaders. An active and concerted plan for leader development and mentorship is essential to growth, profitability, and ethical business conduct. Money invested in effective leader development will provide a return that boosts the bottom line.

4 Power Thoughts

1. Think about the leaders you have personally met. What qualities do you value most about them?
2. Do you strive to embody the qualities of a positive leader in your character?
3. Do you feel that the leadership at your current employer is effective?
4. Have you ever benefited from a positive mentor/mentee relationship?
5. What obstacles have you encountered that inhibit your personal leadership growth?

CHAPTER 3

Calling All Mentors!

"We make a living by what we get, we make a life by what we give."

– Winston Churchill

M entorship is the most effective way of transferring skills to the next generation of top performers. Imagine yourself as an aspiring real estate developer sitting down with Donald Trump for a few hours every week to learn his master strategies. What if you wanted to become an expert investor and could have Warren Buffett as your mentor? I'm sure you agree that these would be powerful opportunities to learn about real estate development and investing. What if you could do the same with a great leader? Wouldn't that also provide a powerful opportunity to learn about leadership?

Becoming a capable leader depends on your ability to develop a range of skills. Every leader would benefit from learning these skills firsthand from another accomplished leader. In finding a mentor, ideally you want someone who is trusted, respected, and can impart wisdom based not only on their professional life, but their personal life as well. Studies have shown that one of the best ways to develop as a leader is through observing effective leaders and developing a relationship with a mentor.

Informal Mentoring

What can you do when a formal mentor is not readily available? In the previous chapter, I discussed specific obstacles that inhibit the establishment of productive mentor/mentee relationships. If you take on the attitude of a committed leadership student, you can overcome the lack of formal mentorship by modeling other successful leaders. In effect, modeling is mentorship through observation. Leadership modeling is simply a methodical observation of the success patterns used by great leaders. Modeling can be applied both to leaders that you have direct contact with and great leaders that you study. It can be an effective substitute when direct mentoring in not an available option. It also circumvents many of the obstacles to one-on-one meetings between mentors and mentees.

Everyone learns through observation of others to some degree. However, we often begin to emulate those around us with little regard to whether the behavior being emulated is optimal. Modeling differs from mere mimicking of those around us. When you model effectively, you deliberately filter and analyze all observations. You have to assess the actions of the leaders you're studying for effectiveness.

To apply modeling as a substitute for direct mentoring, you select one or more senior leaders with whom you interact on a regular basis. You then conduct a detailed study of the senior leaders' approach to leadership by scrutinizing everything they do. Analyze why they did it and assess the results. (You can apply the 4 Power Leadership Framework, which you will learn about shortly, as a tool in assessing the leader's effectiveness.) In effect, you establish an informal mentoring relationship that can result in powerful knowledge transfer, while maintaining a comfortable distance between you and the mentor. This approach allows you to learn from people whom you believe are better skilled and more experienced in the craft of leadership than yourself. You can ask probing questions to seek clarification and understanding without revealing your underlying purpose or burdening the leader with the possibly unwanted role of mentor.

Modeling can be a very effective way to learn as long as it is accompanied with a conscious analysis of the leader's effectiveness. It can also save you a great deal of learning time because it can be readily applied simultaneously to multiple leaders you wish to study. Modeling provides an opportunity for you to graft the best qualities and methods of other leaders onto your own personality and repertoire of techniques.

You should select your mentors carefully to avoid wasting valuable learning time. Remember, no one is perfect and everyone has his or her flaws. Therefore, don't go "all in" assuming any particular person is the perfect leader and possesses all the right qualities and methods. You should identify the strengths of those you model and avoid their weaknesses. Adopt the qualities that are compatible with the positive philosophy of *4 Power Leadership*.

Model the Greatest

Sometimes you may find that the leaders around you are mediocre and too ineffective to serve as informal mentors. The leaders you have access to may even be negative role models that you should avoid. Modeling can still be successful by applying the technique to leaders from the past or current public figures you can study. In fact, studying leadership excellence through the ages is highly recommended whether you have ready access to good mentorship sources or not. You can turn these distant public figures into virtual mentors by engaging in an in-depth study of their lives. When you have full appreciation of their lives, your virtual mentors become much more than superficial role models.

In selecting historic persons and public figures for modeling as virtual mentors, I look for people who faced extraordinary circumstances that tested their character as leaders. There are plenty of historic figures, including poets and scientists, who have extraordinary accomplishments to their credit but are simply not classified as leaders. While you can glean tremendous wisdom and insight from these historic figures, they're not leadership models for everyday needs.

There are some interesting advantages to modeling past leaders. Broadening your exposure to leaders across history gives you a sense of what leadership was like through the ages. This will expose you to a multitude of situations and motivational approaches. You will see patterns emerge among those you study, and there are no limitations on who you can model because you have access to online information on every great leader.

Studying contemporary public figures is essential as well because relating to them within the framework of the times in which we live provides more immediate context for their leadership actions. However, the image of contemporary figures is often surrounded by "noise" that their proponents and opponents generate for a variety of reasons – many of them self-serving. The noise consists of both unwarranted criticism and unwarranted praise. The passage of time has a way of dialing down the noise that surrounds the name of prominent people yielding a more balanced scorecard of their contributions.

As J. Christopher Herold so eloquently said in his book, *The Age of Napoleon*:

"History experienced and history remembered are two different things."

Through the decades or even centuries, the most significant accomplishments and most significant detractors of historic figures will float to the top. In some cases, it takes a great deal of time for the decisions they made to be proven right or wrong. Ultimately, the irrelevant is relegated to obscurity, and the significant becomes more pronounced, providing a more balanced perspective of their impact.

In looking to historic figures as virtual mentors, you may argue that selecting people who are not our contemporaries makes their leadership lessons less relevant to today's students. In fact, the lessons of history are invaluable. They not only teach us what works, but just as importantly what doesn't. In leadership, avoiding the mistakes of the past is as valuable as knowing what to do in the present.

All great leaders share an important common thread. They were all extraordinary students of human nature. Their leadership acuity was undoubtedly derived from their ability to read the situations they encountered in terms of the motivations of those they led and those they opposed. Human nature has not changed despite the relentless passage of time – and likely never will.

In studying past prominent leaders, you should compile a list of your favorite people who have standout qualities and rose to a level of great historic significance. The eclectic list below provides inspiration for sources of virtual mentorship.

Historic Figures	Sports
Abraham Lincoln	Vince Lombardi
George Washington	
Thomas Jefferson	**Business**
John Adams	Jack Welch
Benjamin Franklin	Steve Jobs
Mohandas Gandhi	
Winston Churchill	**World Leaders**
Elizabeth I	Margaret Thatcher
Julius Caesar	
Napoleon Bonaparte	**Religious Figures**
	Mother Teresa

The list ranges from people of virtually unassailable character to those who may be seen as somewhat controversial. This list is not intended to be exhaustive or definitive by any means. I encourage you to modify it to suit your needs, or to make your own personal list entirely from scratch. The main point is to have a list of proven and effective leaders who can serve as virtual mentors that you can model in developing specific facets of your leadership ability.

To be of value as a virtual mentor, each person you select must meet three criteria. First, each leader must have standout characteristics that you can easily identify. Second, the leader's characteristics should serve to immediately improve your leadership effectiveness. Third, the leader's attributes should be a source of inspiration and guidance when you are confronted with challenges throughout your career. For example, if you want to learn first- class leadership oratory, then study Lincoln and Churchill. If you want to enhance your skills in bold, strategic, and tactical thinking, then study Napoleon and Caesar. If you want to enhance your skills in building rapport and swaying the opinions of others, then you should study Jefferson and Franklin. Get the idea?

The role of gender is not very significant when examining leadership qualities. Both genders are capable of moving mountains through the application of sound leadership skills. Selecting effective leaders from both genders further diversifies your learning perspective.

As you judge the leadership qualities of adopted historic mentors from this list or your own, be sure to judge them in context and as products of their times. This is very important. While virtues are timeless, circumstances and customs of bygone eras often lead to actions that we would find objectionable or beyond the socially accepted norms of our present time. To pull a historic figure forward in time and judge their characters solely in the context of today's culture is simplistic revisionism.

Full understanding of your historic mentor's true character requires in-depth study of his life in context of his era. Reading autobiographies, when available, in combination with reputable biographies is the recommended way to learn the true essence of these individuals. An autobiography provides direct insight into the mind of the mentor. Following up by reading a reputable biography helps to round out the picture since autobiographies aren't generally self-critical. Reading both autobiographies and biographies provides a balanced perspective and can also show how the subject's contemporaries viewed the person.

After studying the lives of the people on your list, their personas will come to life. You will feel as if you personally know them. Put them to work for you. Ask questions. What qualities did Lincoln display that would help me in my situation? What qualities can I draw from Napoleon as I try to out-maneuver a competitor in achieving my goal? The goal is not to become a parrot of someone from the past but to channel effective leadership qualities from the masters who have proven their worth to the world.

American readers don't have to look very far for brilliant examples of leadership that can be emulated in developing one's leadership core. Some leadership standouts in our history are Abraham Lincoln and the founding fathers, Washington, Jefferson, Adams, and Franklin. Non-American readers can take this opportunity to learn about America's roots.

Abraham Lincoln is viewed by many historians as the greatest president America has ever had. However, as with all leaders, Lincoln was reviled and ridiculed by his rivals, lampooned in the press as a baboon, and criticized for his physical appearance. Of course, he was also despised throughout the Confederacy for his opposition to slavery and secession. However, when viewed through the eyes of posterity, almost everyone would agree that his faith, patience, integrity, and perseverance are the core reasons why the United States still exists as a united country.

An effective leader must be able to clearly communicate his vision, plans, and inspiration. Lincoln possessed extraordinary speech-writing and oratory talent that he used skillfully. His Gettysburg Address endures today as one of the most profound and moving speeches.

There are people in the world who are seemingly chosen by God to bear a disproportionately great burden on behalf of the rest of us at just the right time. The tasks they face, even to them, seem so unbearable that the way forward appears dark and the goal, at times, unattainable. Yet it is the very burden they bear at their great moment in human history that causes them to rise to the challenge. Somehow they persist. Somehow they succeed. Lincoln was such a leader. Lincoln's character endures as one of high virtue and selflessness.

George Washington is synonymous with leadership presence. The confidence and calm with which he carried himself was a continuous source of inspiration to his troops during the darkest times of the American Revolutionary War. Washington was universally admired for his courage and leadership presence in leading the rag-tag Continental Army against a much more disciplined and better-equipped British Army. Washington's tenacity enabled him to turn disaster into success.

At the conclusion of the war, European allies and suspicious factions in the United States feared that Washington would morph into an American Caesar and assume emperor status. Washington, however, resigned his post as Commander in Chief of the Continental Army. His yielding of authority before Congress established the American tradition of civilian control of the military. Later elected unanimously by the Electoral College as the first president of the fledgling United States, Washington once more demonstrated his unwavering virtue as he again relinquished power after his second term in office. These two extraordinary demonstrations of his virtuous leadership core solidified his stature in American history and garnered widespread admiration that endures to this present day.

Thomas Jefferson was the most eloquent writer among the founding fathers and was selected to author the Declaration of Independence by the Second Continental Congress. He penned the immortal words in the Declaration:

> *"We hold these truths to be self-evident, that all men are created equal, that they are endowed by their Creator with certain unalienable Rights, that among these are Life, Liberty and the pursuit of Happiness."*

He served the country as a member of the Continental Congress, state legislator, Governor of Virginia, diplomat, and as the third President of the United States.

Jefferson enjoyed a high degree of public adulation both at home and overseas during his tenure as a diplomat in France. He often wielded his power and influence through third parties in behind-the-scenes power plays. This technique allowed him to avoid many public confrontations with adversaries until it was too late for them to stop his initiatives. Publicly, Jefferson always maintained extraordinary self-control. His keen understanding of human nature was instrumental in shaping the ideals of a young nation. His prudence and wisdom enabled him to skillfully navigate through tenuous international relations during the country's early years. His skillful leadership positioned him to later take bold action in purchasing the Louisiana territory, which doubled the size of the country.

John Adams was America's brilliant and highly principled second president. One of his key leadership skills was a consistent ability to spot the right talent. Throughout his career, he had a knack for recommending the right person for a critical job. He persuaded the Committee on Independence to select Jefferson as the author of the Declaration of Independence. Later, the Continental Congress unanimously appointed Washington as Commander in Chief, also on the recommendation of John Adams.

Adams was known for his resolute, blunt, and direct style. This leadership style stood in stark contrast to that of Franklin and Jefferson who often chafed at his approach on a variety of issues. However, Adams' leadership style had effective uses as well. He was a prominent leader in the Continental Congress when the decision to declare independence from Britain was made. He resisted any talk of reconciliation with Britain when the Revolution was going badly. Adams was resolute in his beliefs, even when he was met with overwhelming opposition. Sometimes this trait was seen as petty stubbornness when he would incessantly debate seemingly innocuous issues. However, when it mattered most, his resoluteness proved valuable.

During his administration, his stubbornness in not yielding to calls for confrontation with France averted war with the former ally. Despite overwhelming popular sentiment to declare war and seek revenge for violations of America's sovereignty, Adams stood his ground. Avoidance of this war saved the nation from near certain bankruptcy. More importantly, the avoidance of hostilities with France later paved the way for Jefferson to execute the Louisiana Purchase during his administration. Patience pays.

Benjamin Franklin had a long and distinguished life's journey from his humble beginnings as a printer's apprentice to diplomat. He was a successful businessman, printer, publisher, inventor, and statesman earning honorary degrees from both Harvard and Yale.

Franklin is the only one of the founding fathers who signed all four documents that marked the founding of the United States: the Declaration of Independence (1776); the Treaty of Alliance, Amity, and Commerce with France (1778); the Treaty of Peace between England, France, and the United States (1782); and the Constitution (1787). He also assisted in writing and editing parts of the Declaration of Independence and the Constitution.

Franklin was beloved in France. In fact, for a while his popularity there even exceeded his popularity in America. He adroitly exploited his status as a celebrity and became a powerful influencer in French political circles. His popularity was a major factor in obtaining key loans and popular support for the American cause. He persuaded the French to form an alliance with America and enter the American war for independence in opposition to the British.

Franklin was the originator of the "ask it, don't tell it" style of leadership. Early in his public life, he found that if he stated a position, he would become a lightning rod for attack and would be compelled to defend his position. Being all too acquainted with the function of lightning rods, he devised a unique style instead. He would patiently listen to all sides of an argument, and at the right moment ask key questions that would cause people to refine or rethink their arguments and positions. This leadership style resulted in him being viewed as patient, wise, and non-confrontational. Since he rarely argued publicly with his peers, he became a very popular and trusted sage whose wisdom was indispensable when important decisions had to be made. Franklin derived his style from his study of the Socratic method, which can be learned by reading the Five Dialogues of Plato.

Winston Churchill's leadership is distinguished for his unwavering resistance in the face of the advancing Nazi war machine. Churchill stands shoulder to shoulder with Lincoln as one of the two masters of all time in leadership oratory. During the darkest hours of World War II, the British endured relentless German bombardments. At times, it seemed all that stood between Britain and oblivion was the sound of Churchill's voice. This is exemplified by his speech before the House of Commons on June 4, 1940:

> *"We shall go on to the end, we shall fight in France, we shall fight on the seas and oceans, we shall fight with growing confidence and growing strength in the air, we shall defend our Island, whatever the cost may be, we shall fight on the beaches, we shall fight on the landing grounds, we shall fight in the fields and in the streets, we shall fight in the hills; we shall never surrender..."*

Tenacity and persistence pays off. Churchill's inspirational leadership style and skills as an orator and speechwriter qualify him as mandatory study for anyone with leadership aspirations.

Mohandas Gandhi liberated the Indian people by gaining India's independence from the British Empire simply through the power of his words without ever firing a shot or inciting people to violence. He freed millions from subjugation through the organization of civil disobedience and passive resistance campaigns. His peaceful tactics brought an empire to its knees and forced Britain to relinquish control of India. Not only is his leadership distinguished by his peaceful resistance tactics, but also by his persistence and incomparable discipline in pursuing his worthy goal of freedom for the Indian people. Gandhi's tactics would later serve as a blueprint for Martin Luther King Jr.'s strategy during the American Civil Rights movement. Gandhi's determined leadership style is best summarized in his own words. Leaders who wish to inspire followers to a cause often use this simple quote:

"First they ignore you, then they mock you, then they fight you, then you win."

Despite Gandhi's relentless and selfless efforts, Indian independence brought Gandhi little joy. As British rule began to lose its grip, sectarian violence spiraled out of control. Indian society erupted in massive riots and commission of atrocities between Muslims and Hindus. While Gandhi consistently preached against hatred, his opponents readily gave into it and later assassinated him. Prior to his death, Gandhi left these inspirational words for every aspiring leader to live by:

"Whenever you are in doubt, or when the self becomes too much with you, apply the following test. Recall the face of the poorest and the weakest man whom you may have seen, and ask yourself, if the step you contemplate is going to be of any use to him. Will he gain anything by it? Will it restore him to a control over his own life and destiny? In other words, will it lead

to swaraj [freedom] for the hungry and spiritually starving millions? Then you will find your doubts and yourself melt away."

Interestingly, Churchill and Gandhi were adversaries. Churchill was a strong believer in the British Empire and resisted any thought of Indian independence. Each man was a hero to his culture for specific reasons at specific times. Their opposition is testimony to the complexities leaders encounter and how each leader rises in accordance with the challenges of the times. Success is often ultimately determined by the degree of alignment of one's cause with virtue.

How could Churchill, who was so right as the champion of freedom in his fight against the Nazis, be so wrong in his denial of freedom for the Indian people? A similar paradox looms as a shadow over the magnificent legacies of Washington and Jefferson, who were both slaveholders. Yet, they both fought for freedom and enshrined its universal principles in the annals of human history. They laid the foundations for a nation that ultimately could no longer tolerate slavery. Leaders often exhibit such paradoxes. To dismiss them entirely for their errors is as wrong as accepting them blindly without scrutiny.

Julius Caesar and Napoleon Bonaparte are two controversial choices on my list of worthy virtual mentors. They both emerged on the scene of their respective periods during times of political and economic turmoil. Both Caesar and Bonaparte succeeded in turning the establishment power base on its head. Historians are split on their respective places in history. To merely dismiss them as self-serving tyrants is an inaccurate portrayal. They are more accurately described as complicated products of their time. Both Caesar and Bonaparte brought about massive change through simultaneously creative and destructive force. Though both were driven by great personal ambition, neither was driven by hate.

David Potter describes Caesar's leadership characteristics in his book, *The Emperors of Rome*:

> *"...boundless capacity for forward planning, a keen understanding of the psychology of his opponents, and impressive flexibility when confronted with new problems, and a profound confidence in his own ability."*

Caesar was the embodiment of the Roman virtue of *gravitas* – a critical leadership characteristic defined as personal bearing that projects importance without arrogance.

Napoleon came to power at the tail end of the French Revolution, restoring social order and bringing the endless purges and executions of that bloody period to a close. He left a legacy of social and governmental reform, including the rebuilding of administrations, the introduction of the metric system, and his most lasting legacy, the Napoleonic Code, which reshaped European society. To study Napoleon is to conduct a study of inspirational leadership through which he often achieved military victories against vastly superior forces. He was a superb strategist and leveraged his predominant characteristics of decisiveness and speed to action.

Elizabeth I is distinguished as one of history's most popular monarchs who reigned during what is considered the Golden Age of English history. She was the daughter of Henry VIII and his second wife, Ann Boleyn. Henry VIII's machinations surrounding his desire to produce a male heir constitute a story of their own. For our purposes, it suffices to know that Elizabeth's birth was a great disappointment to Henry. He promptly had her declared illegitimate with regard to her place in succeeding to the throne. Her childhood was difficult, but she was nevertheless given a first-class education.

In 1558, the unwanted daughter of a king finally succeeded in ascending to the throne. Through her shrewd maneuvering in male-dominated circles of other contemporary monarchies, she proved to be an extremely capable, dedicated, and popular queen.

Her leadership ability is distinguished by a talent for selecting trustworthy advisors and an ability to select the proper course of action based on the advice she received. She also demonstrated flexibility in adjusting unpopular policies without allowing her ego to interfere with sound decision making. She successfully transformed England from a strife-torn, impoverished nation to one of the most powerful and wealthy nations on earth at the time of her death in 1603.

Margaret Thatcher, the Iron Lady, became the first female prime minister of Great Britain. She won three successive terms, serving more than eleven years. She rose to power at a time when Great Britain faced accelerating economic decline and complex geopolitical threats. Mrs. Thatcher was successful in introducing badly needed economic reforms and in reversing Britain's shrinking influence in world affairs. Her steadfast leadership and reinvigorated alliance with the United States were instrumental in pushing the crumbling Soviet Empire over the edge and bringing the Cold War to an end.

Margaret Thatcher's tenure helped give her nation a renewed sense of vitality. Her standout characteristics are clearly her resolve and adherence to her principles. Her ability to project a powerful leadership presence while preserving a "feminine" image is an example of the delicate balancing act that many women leaders face. Mrs. Thatcher pulled it off and can serve as an example for female leaders in this regard.

Mrs. Thatcher, who passed away in April 2013, is definitely surrounded by the "noise" of current politics. Depending on your ideological bent, she is either a heroine or a reviled politician.

However, there is no question that Margaret Thatcher was transformative whether you agree or disagree with her politics.

Mother Teresa's leadership in charitable work is a true example of do-as-I-do leadership. Modern-day, secularized political correctness may cause you to shy away from studying her life. You don't have to join a convent or convert to Catholicism to examine her life and contributions to humanity. Study of Mother Teresa's life provides leadership lessons on lifting and comforting the human soul in its darkest moments. Inspiration is the leader's currency, and she was a veritable mint.

The modest beginnings of Mother Teresa's work as a missionary in Calcutta grew into a global relief system serving the poorest of the poor in over 100 countries by the time of her death. Her example as a selfless leader attracted the charitable donations of millions of people around the world. Mother Teresa's ability to organize such a vast assistance operation certainly distinguishes her as one of history's great leaders. Yet even her selflessness did not escape criticism. Criticism goes with the territory of being a leader. It's always much easier to stand on the sidelines and throw rocks than it is to get out front and lead. Mother Teresa's writings and quotations are a source of spiritual inspiration when a leader may be facing hardships and the way forward is obscured.

Vince Lombardi was the legendary coach of the Green Bay Packers football team. By the time he took over as head coach and general manager in 1959, the once-vaunted Green Bay Packers, who had won six National Football League Championships, had fallen on hard times. Lombardi had second thoughts about accepting his position because the struggling franchise had grown to expect mediocrity and failure. By his second year, the Packers were back in the championship game though they lost. By his third year, they won their first NFL Championship under his leadership. It would be the first of five championships in seven years under Lombardi.

Lombardi practically willed his teams to victory through the force of his personality and the discipline he instilled in all his players. That discipline is best reflected in the following Lombardi quote:

> *"Perfection is not attainable, but if we chase perfection we can catch excellence."*

His teams did indeed chase perfection. The amount of repetition he would require in practices was legendary. He wanted his players to be able to run plays in their sleep. While he was a stern disciplinarian, his players respected him. He was the quintessential, authentic leader who cared deeply about his players. He remains one of the most quotable and inspirational sources of leadership wisdom to this day.

Jack Welch can easily be named the Vince Lombardi of the corporate world. In fact, similar recognition was bestowed upon him in 1999 when Fortune magazine named Welch "Manager of the Century." The recognition was well earned for his remarkable performance during his tenure as CEO of General Electric (GE) from 1981 to 2001. From his arrival to his last full year with GE in 2000, GE grew its annual revenues from $26.8B to $129.8B.

Welch's leadership style was candid and blunt. He detested bureaucracy and immediately upon the start of his tenure as chairman, began to dismantle it. He empowered junior managers and instilled a culture of nimbleness in what had become a slow, plodding beast.

Welch was bold in his initiatives. He sold off traditional GE businesses in which GE could no longer compete effectively. Welch insisted that GE must be either #1 or #2 in every business

GE owned. If a business could not meet those criteria, it would be sold or shut down.

Welch is not without his detractors. The most consistent criticism has been his downsizing initiatives in which approximately 81,000 employees were let go over the years as he restructured the company. Welch defends his actions as necessary for the health and survival of the company, during a period of dramatically shifting global competitive forces. In retrospect, he was right. Such is the mantle of leadership – unpleasant and sometimes unpopular decisions go with the territory.

Steve Jobs was on a mission to change the world from the first day he and his partner Steve Wozniak decided to start a computer company, later known as Apple, in his parents' garage. That mission drove him onward and upward for the rest of his professional life. Jobs was not known as the most pleasant person to work for. In fact, working for him could be downright harrowing. He was extremely demanding in his pursuit of excellence, and his drive could grind people up in the process.

Jobs consistently held an acutely focused view of the world through the customer's eyes. The products Apple created simply had to comply with that vision, or he could become very unpleasant. Though his leadership style could be abrasive, there is no doubt that his ability to see and create a new future was his most remarkable leadership characteristic. The force of his personality was relentless, and he had little difficulty in persuading others to adopt his vision. That vision built a technological empire.

Mentorship Recap

I hope these snippets from history have inspired you to study the lives of extraordinary leaders. Studying the lives of leaders from the distant and recent past is a valuable source of leadership learning that you should not ignore.

Mentorship is vital to the growth and development of successive generations of leaders. If you have a great leader available to teach you, consider yourself blessed. If you don't have a good mentor you can turn to, don't let that hold you back. Observe, analyze, and model the effective leaders with whom you come in contact in the normal course of your professional life. You can also pick your favorite leaders from history, learn everything you can about them, analyze their effectiveness, and model their successful traits. Adopt virtual mentorship as a valuable learning method.

Regardless of the mentorship source, extracting the good qualities and techniques while discarding the undesirable is the key to getting the most out of mentorship. With the proper filter applied, the dedicated leadership student can easily discern what works and what doesn't.

Leadership is a lifelong journey that will be marked with challenges but will also return a deep sense of fulfillment. *Let your life be distinguished not just by what you give as a leader, but also by what you give to someone else as a mentor.*

4 Power Thoughts

1. Do you have a mentor?
2. Do the leaders you have access to regularly serve as good role models in the study of leadership?
3. What kind of mentors do you feel you need in your current situation and leadership skill level?
4. Make a list of those you would select as historic mentors.
5. Why do the people you selected stand out as leaders?

CHAPTER 4

Leadership Made Simple

"Great leaders are almost always great simplifiers, who can cut through argument, debate, and doubt, to offer a solution everybody can understand."

– Colin Powell

I f great leadership is improved by simplification, then there should also be a simple model for developing leaders. The 4 Power Leadership Framework is exactly that. It is a guide that anyone can understand, easily commit to memory, and implement on a daily basis.

There's been a great deal of research and writing about leadership rules, laws, techniques, methods, principles, and more. But effective leadership remains difficult to create because it is rooted in the intangible. The intangible is the spirit within you, the aspiring leader.

Simply assessing someone's leadership knowledge is not enough to determine their leadership ability. Leadership caliber is hugely dependent on the character of each individual leader. You can only determine leadership effectiveness when someone's knowledge and character are evaluated in combination. That's why it makes perfect sense for you to analyze and perfect your character to the greatest degree possible. Perfecting your character is a key component of the 4 Power Leadership Framework.

The First Power

Personality and character are inner qualities that shape a leader. The study and development of the inner self is the beginning of leadership capability. *Without this most important first step, what you become as a leader will be driven primarily by chance and circumstances over which you have little to no control.* What you become and how you influence others emanates from inside of you. This is why mastery of the inner self is absolutely essential in developing into a well-adjusted complete leader. The study and development of the inner self is explored in *Poise*, the first power of the 4 Power Leadership Framework.

The Second Power

Next, to effectively project your personality as a leader, you must manifest the inner self into an external projection that inspires confidence. Subordinates must see this external projection of your internal leadership core as worthy of respect. Once accepted, your subordinates can commit to you as a respected leader. The external manifestation of the inner self is most fittingly described as a mere image. It is impossible to completely know someone else's inner person. We only see an image of what that inner self shows us, regardless of whether the external image is projected consciously or unconsciously. To lead effectively, you must learn to project your leadership image consciously with specific purpose. The purposeful external projection of the inner self is the second power of the 4 Power Framework – *Presence*.

The Third Power

Accomplishment is the central purpose of leadership. Without a definitive aim in mind, leadership has no purpose and no function. The third power, *Performance*, is the set of leadership qualities, behaviors, and methods that determine a leader's overall effectiveness in achieving results.

The Fourth Power

Many talented and brilliant people have failed in the pursuit of their life's ambitions. Often their failure was not due to a lack of talent or an effective plan. It also was not necessarily due to a lack of development of the three previously described leadership powers. Failure is often "snatched from the jaws of victory" due to an undeveloped fourth power – *Persistence.* Leadership requires tenacity – a conviction that one's cause or endeavor will succeed. Leadership demands determination and the prudence to apply course corrections along the way that will effectively overcome unexpected obstacles. I call persistence the fuel for achievement. It is the leader's tenacity that pushes an organization to achieve its goals especially in those dark moments when success seems most elusive.

Situations Matter

The 4 Power Leadership Framework provides a structure to learn and develop general leadership effectiveness. However, the requirements of a given leadership situation are also a crucial consideration in selecting the right leader for the right job at the right time. A leader who is right for one set of circumstances may be the wrong choice for a different set of circumstances. Subject-matter knowledge must be considered in addition to core leadership skills in selecting a leader for ultimate success. Here's a simple example from my career that illustrates this point.

During my military service, I was assigned to run a data center for an operational testing agency. I was totally in my element. Having recently graduated with an engineering degree, I had the knowledge, skills, and ability required to lead my team in delivering critical data services in support of the greater organization. Conversely, my friend Mark, a peer and fellow lieutenant, was out of his element. He did not have a technical degree and knew very little about data processing. His lack of knowledge made him feel tentative and incapable of developing a vision for our projects. Mark's lack of subject-matter knowledge directly impacted his ability to lead our team.

However, when I visited my other peer lieutenants in tactical units with whom we worked, I was out of my element. They knew all the details of establishing communications systems in operational environments. I simply had not reinforced my training in this area sufficiently to lead effectively. Functional knowledge and experience are essential to leadership success. Leaders must be matched to the requirements of a situation to enhance the chances of a successful outcome.

Assess Your Powers Regularly

Your leadership capacity is determined by the sum of your personality, character, ability, knowledge, and tenacity. Leadership effectiveness is succinctly measured by assessing the 4 Powers. There are only four things that a leader must remember as a gauge for leadership self-improvement. The leader must measure and monitor his effectiveness against the strength of his 4 Powers:

Poise – Am I in control of myself by keeping my emotions in check and my commitment to virtue strong?

Presence – Am I projecting a leadership persona that encourages my subordinates to have faith in my leadership and remain inspired?

Performance – Do I possess the subject-matter knowledge, skills, and plan that will result in success for those I lead?

Persistence – Do I have the tenacity and fortitude required to fight through difficulties?

Finally, two leaders could both have strongly developed powers within the 4 Power Leadership Framework. One may be the right choice and one may not. Relevant experience is the key final criteria in determining ultimate success.

---

4 Power Thoughts

1. Think of a leader you know personally. Assess that leader's effectiveness in the 4 Power Leadership Framework – Poise, Presence, Performance, and Persistence.

2. Assess your own leadership effectiveness in terms of the 4 Power Leadership Framework. Which of the four powers do you feel need the most strengthening?

Section 1
Poise

CHAPTER 5

Poise: The First Power

"Leadership is a matter of having people look at you and gain confidence, seeing how you react. If you're in control, they're in control."

- Tom Landry

L eaders are frequently described as having poise. Widely accepted definitions of poise include:[1]

1. a dignified, self-confident manner or bearing; composure; self-possession: to show poise in company.

2. steadiness; stability: intellectual poise.

Of all the words used to describe poise in this definition, the term that stands out the most to me is "self-possession." Self-possession is the very essence of poise and matches the core concept of a leader that's in control of himself. Self-possession also captures a sense of self-knowledge regarding strengths and weaknesses. Self-possession requires that you be fully conscious of your inner being and thought processes. Without full knowledge of your inner self, it is difficult to control and focus the external projection of your leadership qualities. As Harry Truman observed quite aptly:

---

[1] Merrriam-Webster online and Dictionary.com

"In reading the lives of great men, I found that the first victory they won was over themselves...self-discipline with all of them came first."

President Truman was astutely observing that leadership begins with the mastery of the inner self through self-control. Self-control in turn yields the quality of self-possession, leading to full ownership of your emotions and ultimately resulting in the Power of Poise.

What you project externally comes from who you are internally. The fully poised leader must have an inner self that is understood, composed, nurtured, and directed with purpose in order for his external self to project the proper leadership impact.

Researchers and authors Kouzes and Posner conducted an extensive survey that sought to identify qualities people value most in a leader. Self-control consistently posts last or near last in the survey results; nonetheless it is the most important foundational leadership element from the 4 Power Leadership Framework perspective.

In reality, the two perspectives are not in contradiction. In the Kouzes and Posner survey, respondents are reacting to a question that requires them to rank leadership qualities. The leadership qualities in the survey are cumulative in some aspects and interdependent in other aspects. I don't interpret them all as equal qualities. Additionally, people react to the qualities that will most immediately affect them. Honesty, for example, is most important to respondents because it will have the most profound impact on the leader-subordinate relationship. Therefore, it is not surprising that honesty consistently appears first in survey results.

The self-control aspect of leadership can be likened to the foundation of a house. If you were asked to rank the qualities you valued most in a house, you probably wouldn't say, "A good solid foundation!" Most likely you would say things like "roomy, comfortable, warm, open floor plan," etc. Foundations are essential but unseen. However, just as you cannot build a house without a strong foundation, self-control is the foundational element that gives the leader his Power of Poise. Leadership that is built to last is built upon self-control.

Let's examine further why the inner self is so relevant to effective leadership. The internally conflicted and insecure leader will have difficulty in achieving sustainable, long-term success. Followers will inherently sense the leader's internal conflicts, and he will be ineffective because other people will not be able to commit to him and accept his leadership. Unless the leader masters his internal challenges and wins the victory over "self" first, he will lack the solid inner core upon which leadership is built. To positively impact other people, you must set things right internally first.

If you aren't comfortable in your own skin and you lack the sense of self-possession that accompanies the Power of Poise, take heart. Like most aspects of your life, you have the power to change. Necessary internal adjustments can be achieved through a process of deep introspection. The pioneering psychologist, Abraham Maslow, believed that:

> *"What is necessary to change a person is to change his awareness of himself."*

Maslow advanced therapies in applied psychology that leveraged the inner tools that people have to heal emotional wounds and rebalance their disposition. It is a philosophy of empowerment through self-knowledge.

A leader, by the very essence of his position, will attract the full and constant scrutiny of others. If you don't fully understand yourself, you will be at a severe disadvantage as a leader. People will ultimately know your strengths and weaknesses better than you do. The journey toward developing the Power of Poise will take you through a process that will create much fuller self-knowledge. Through self-knowledge, you can then make needed adjustments. Through focus, attention, and repetitive effort, self-control can be fortified.

---

4 Power Thoughts

1. Where is your moral center?
   a. What is your personal code of ethics?
   b. Is it good for the people you lead?
   c. What adjustments do you need to make?
2. What are your top three strengths?
   a. How can you exploit these strengths to the maximum extent possible?
3. What are your top three weaknesses?
   a. What good habits can you introduce to counter your weaknesses?
   b. What types of people do you need around you to compensate for your weaknesses and complement your strengths?
4. What kind of emotional baggage are you carrying around?
   a. Can you lead effectively with this baggage?

CHAPTER 6

Do You Have the
Right Moral Center?

"All great things are simple, and many can be expressed in single words: freedom, justice, honor, duty, mercy, hope."

– *Winston Churchill*

V irtue is a state of moral excellence as defined by a set of superior moral qualities. Virtue also alludes to a way of life in which you behave in accordance with these high moral qualities.

The Study of Virtue

The study of virtue in Western civilization can be traced as far back as the mid-fifth century B.C. Around 380 B.C., the Greek philosopher Plato first defined the four cardinal virtues of *temperance, prudence, fortitude, and justice.* Virtue as a way of life arose from his study of what sets a human apart from a brute and establishes a superior character. One of the *Five Dialogues of Plato* entitled, *Meno,* is almost entirely devoted to the discussion of virtue. It is also a good introduction to the method of relentless questioning employed by Socrates, the central figure of the dialogues. This method is known today as the Socratic Method. The *Meno* dialogue is likely the historical collection of thought that launched virtue as a formal discipline of study.

As a concerned philosopher, Socrates was appalled by the moral decay of Greek society at the time. He accused the Sophists of promoting a form of moral relativism that he saw as contributing to this decay. Their central principles furthered the belief that there is no objective standard of true and false. Consequently, Socrates saw the extension of the Sophists' thought to also include that there is no objective standard of good, which in turn leads to moral chaos. He sought to reverse this philosophical trend by embarking on a search for knowledge about virtue.

In the dialogue, Socrates examines whether virtue can be taught and the relationship of knowledge to virtue. He establishes two points. First, conventional knowledge about a subject so fundamental as virtue requires questioning and deep introspection. Second, virtue is as much dependent on individual internal commitment and acceptance as it is on knowledge and wisdom.

The next major milestone in the study of virtues is the work of Aristotle between 334 and 323 B.C. During this time he wrote his treatise, *Ethics*, forming the foundation of Western thought on the subject of virtues. There are four central themes in Ethics that have direct correlation to virtue in leadership.

The purpose of virtue is happiness. Ultimately, the fundamental human desire is to be happy. Aristotle saw happiness as the ultimate result of a virtuous life.

Virtues are created by habit. Studying virtue will make you aware of its existence and applicability, but virtue is only learned by practice and developing habits consistent with virtue.

Virtues are not absolute. In his *Doctrine of the Mean*, Aristotle presented the idea that virtue lies between two extremes. In effect, every virtue can become a vice if it is taken to an extreme of excess or deficit. Examining the extremes of fortitude provides a simple example. Excessive fortitude becomes recklessness or rashness. Deficit of fortitude becomes cowardice. The extremes of recklessness and cowardice are considered vices according to Aristotle. Virtue is therefore a mean between the two. Aristotle's use of the word "mean" does not imply an exact empirical average, but that prudence must be applied to determine the virtuous path between the extreme of two vices.

One must pursue all virtues. In order for a person to be considered virtuous, he must possess all the virtues. Aristotle referred to this as *unity of virtues.*

Flashing forward in history to 146 B.C., the Roman conquest of the Greek peninsula was by then completed. The ancient Romans had a system of assimilating the cultures of conquered lands by grafting the best characteristics of these cultures into their own. Roman intellectual circles developed a clearly defined discipline of virtue, which they adopted from the Greeks. The Roman virtues were integrated as a way of life for the educated classes. The formalization of the Roman code of virtues became the guidelines by which a Roman citizen was expected to live his life. It was a clear attempt to establish a social structure that permeated society. Here is a sampling of typical Roman virtues:[2]

- **Honesty (Veritas)** – particularly in our dealings with others. The concept that your word is your bond.
- **Dignity (Dignitas)** – a defined sense of self-worth. Personal pride in one's own character and essence.
- **Fortitude (Virtus)** – courage.

---

[2] Researched, cross-referenced, and verified from a variety of dictionaries, encyclopedias, and university sources. Additional references: "Caesar" by Christian Meier; "Moral letters to Lucilius" by Seneca.

- **Gravity (Gravitas)** – seriousness about our dealings and a discernment of the importance of matters at hand.
- **Honor (Honestas)** – integrity, the presentation of oneself as a respectable and contributing member of society.
- **Humanity (Humanitas)** – being educated and instructed, possessing culture and refinement. The idea that one is more than a brute but has the innate capability to lift oneself above the muck.
- **Industriousness (Industria)** – the concept of being resourceful and self-sufficient through one's own hard work.
- **Loyalty (Pietas)** – implies piety in the sense that one has respect for the social, political, and religious order of things to include devotion to one's country and a sense of duty.
- **Sternness (Severitas)** – strictness, self-control.
- **Prudence (Prudentia)** – good sense, wisdom, and discretion. Having the foresight to consider the impact of one's actions before engaging rash decisions.
- **Tenacity (Firmitas)** – firmness, possessing strength of character to stick to one's decisions and pursuits.

After the collapse of the Roman Empire, Aristotelian ethics went through a period of dormancy until the writings of St. Thomas Aquinas revived interest in the latter part of the 12th century.

Values Are Too Arbitrary

Most public corporations have values and ethics policies. The prevailing corporate approach is to focus on regulating the behavior of its employees. Given the damage that ethics breaches can cause to a company, you would think the approach makes sense. Companies have been fined hundreds of millions of dollars because of the moral failings of a few individuals. Sometimes, as in the case of the famous Enron debacle, moral failings can completely collapse a company.

Ethics policies are in effect legal requirements for corporate governance. Usually, they are designed to protect the corporation and are focused on making sure that employees don't do anything illegal. By delineating behavior that is out of bounds, a company establishes legal recourse to dismiss employees who violate policies. Therefore, ethics policies serve an important function, but they don't do enough to shape corporate culture. Ethics policies are usually focused on only one virtue– honesty. That's not a bad thing, but what about all the other virtues that are hugely important in establishing a positive, high-performing corporate culture?

Value statements are extremely arbitrary. Values can be based on anything that someone claims to be important. While many value statements identify some virtues as values, the majority of value statements focus on things that are not classified as virtues. Most corporate value statements will typically cover quality, customer satisfaction, value to shareholders and a general statement about community responsibility. Even with these deficiencies, value statements serve a purpose. They remind employees of their mission and their purpose in serving as an employee of the company. However, value statements generally fall short of reinforcing virtues and their importance to corporate life.

Ethics and values statements are behavior-oriented codes of conduct. *Virtues are essence-oriented and address what a person should strive to be.* By teaching the essence of what creates good conduct and by committing to sound qualities, behavior naturally improves. If someone is virtuous, you don't have to worry about his or her behavior. I developed the *4 Power Leadership – Table of Virtues* (shown below) using Aristotle's *Doctrine of the Mean* to align key leadership virtues to the 4 Powers and to help leaders gauge the consequences of poorly developed virtues.

While it's easy to focus on corporate scandals that highlight moral failures of leadership, there are other reasons why virtues are important as the foundation for corporate culture. The cumulative negative effect on corporate performance when employees don't live up to virtues is a significant drag on the bottom line. Corporate cultures that are not rooted in virtue devolve into internal disharmony and fail to foster positive interaction between employees. Since virtues will have been either learned or not learned by employees prior to joining a corporation, people will enter any given organization with highly varying value systems that are not all necessarily beneficial for the community of employees.

The *4 Power Leadership – Table of Virtues* is the central device by which leaders can achieve common ground on what defines virtuous character. While virtues are more fundamental to moral behavior than values, virtues are not absolutes either. For example, in a given circumstance, people may have varying views on what constitutes justice. However, people can generally agree that someone's conduct has drifted toward deficiency or excess of virtue. The Table of Virtues is useful as a tool for generating discussion about virtue. *As a leader within a corporate culture, the more you discuss and emphasize virtue, the more you will narrow the band of opinion toward a prevailing consensus on what constitutes virtue.*

4 Power Leadership – Table of Virtues

Virtue Definition	Deficiency (Vice)	Virtue	Excess (Vice)
Poise			
Defined sense of self-worth; personal pride in one's own character and essence	Depravity	**Dignity**	Imperiousness
Moderation or self-restraint in action, statement, etc.; self-control	Self-indulgence	**Temperance**	Insensibility
Well-controlled ego	Hubris	**Humility**	Meekness
Presence			
Truthfulness; sincerity	Deceit	**Honesty**	Naiveté
Important, confident, self-assured	Frivolity	**Gravitas**	Arrogance
Integrity in ones beliefs and actions; respectable	Disgrace	**Honor**	Egotism
Learned, educated and in-structed; possessing culture and refinement	Ignorance	**Humanitas**	Pedantry
Performance			
Mental and emotional strength when facing diffi-culty	Cowardice	**Fortitude**	Recklessness
Resourceful and self-sufficient through one's own hard work	Helplessness	**Industriousness**	Isolation
Righteousness, equitable-ness, or moral rightness	Injustice	**Justice**	Injustice
Faithfulness to commitments and obligations; sense of duty	Selfishness	**Loyalty**	Subservience
Good sense, wisdom, and personal discretion; having the foresight to consider the impact of one's actions be-fore engaging rash decisions	Rashness	**Prudence**	Vacillation
Persistence			
Possessing strength of char-acter to stick to one's deci-sions and pursuits	Timidity	**Tenacity**	Obstinance

Promote Corporate Virtue

Leaders can correct a negative culture by promoting a corporate culture that is based on virtue, and above all, acting in a manner that is consistent with virtue. Your virtues must not be compromised when the going gets tough. When a leader embraces virtue, his strong moral center gives him an unassailable position. The strength of his position remains intact as long as the just principles he espouses are not abandoned or violated through his own actions. The more a leader clings to just principles, the stronger his leadership position becomes. When a leader genuinely embraces virtue as his core value, he will quickly earn the loyalty of his following as long as he does not appear "holier than thou." The leader shouldn't be claiming he is perfect. However, he should be steadfast in his commitment to the pursuit of virtue in all dealings. In leadership, you are never off the hook for a moral failing.

When a leader commits a moral transgression, he becomes vulnerable to derision. The leader's detractors will use the transgression to the fullest extent as a means of destroying the leader, whether or not his destruction is justified. Not only will the detractors tear down the leader, but they also tend to tear down the principles to which the leader subscribed. However, failure of a leader to behave virtuously does not mean virtue is invalidated as a core leadership requirement. Doing so is a logical fallacy.

Virtue stands by itself, and the standard bearer is not greater than the standard. If the standard bearer should fall, doesn't the next person in line quickly pick up the standard and press on? This is exactly the code that was followed by the armies of old when they marched bravely into battle holding their standard. In this sense, the standard is a flag or the emblematic symbol of an army or nation. No single individual was considered greater than the whole. No one could stand taller than the standard. The standard would never be left on the ground as long as there was an able-bodied man who could pick it up and carry it forward. Doesn't the same logic hold for our moral standards? Do we abandon all our moral standards merely because a leader fails to live up to them? The standard bearer is not greater than the standard.

Today, the dominant theme in society seems to be that morality, good, and evil are all just relative. The debate between moral relativism and objective morality was raging even in the mid-fourth century B.C. How has relativism worked out through the ages? It has been the justification for all of the most heinous acts perpetrated by humanity. Every leader wants to justify his actions, no matter how heinous. Relativism provides the perfect formula for doing so.

As Aristotle noted, virtue and morality are not exact sciences. However, there is a very important interplay among virtues that helps us to arrive at what is good. The virtue of prudence helps us to discern what is good and where the mean lies with respect to virtue and circumstances. Finally, when in doubt, you have two further tests to help you determine whether you are close to the mean of virtue as Aristotle defined. Test one – Does it pass the test of the Golden Rule, "Do unto others as you would have them do unto you?" Test two – What is the intent of the act? If a leader's action is based on the sincere best interest of others, chances are his carefully weighed decisions will align with true virtue.

We need more leaders who are committed to a higher standard of conduct. We should avoid supporting leaders who do not embrace virtue. We can distinguish between the two types of leaders by the sum of their deeds, while recognizing that no one will be perfect. Advancing the pursuit of virtue as a core leadership attribute among corporate leaders of all levels will clearly move a corporate culture toward higher standards of conduct.

Training in virtues can strengthen leaders' decision making when encountering difficult situations. To support this point, we will briefly examine two recent leadership failures of epic proportions. The first example illustrates how a corporate culture that does not rely on well-developed virtues to make difficult decisions can quickly spin out of control and into disaster. The second example illustrates how poor leadership can take a horrible situation from bad to worse when virtues are not used as the guideposts for crisis management.

Case Study – BP Oil Spill

The first example is the well-known Gulf of Mexico oil spill of April 2010. Through a series of decisions, BP managers abandoned a culture of safety in favor of a culture of cost cutting. There is nothing inherently wrong with reducing costs. Effective leaders should always seek to make their businesses more robust and competitive. The problem arises when the focus on cost cutting overrides all other considerations. This appears to have been the case with BP.

Years before the tragic spill occurred, BP leadership pushed hard to implement aggressive cost cutting across the entire company. They failed to emphasize that cost cutting should not be done at the expense of safety. Instead of a culture that strove for efficiency and safety, BP was gripped by a culture of cutting corners.

During the inquiry on the causes of the Gulf oil spill, a congressional investigation[3] identified five principle causes for the disaster. The common thread to all five causes was a recurring trade-off between safety and cost reduction. The infamous Macondo well was weeks behind schedule and costing BP millions of dollars for each day that it was not in production. The most egregious of the five poor decisions was the failure to run proper testing on the wellhead cement job. BP managers decided to simply skip testing that would verify that the cement job on the wellhead was effective and could indeed prevent dangerous flammable gases from shooting upward into the oil rig.

Sure enough, when an emergency arose and the well had to be sealed due to rising levels of combustible gas, the cement in the wellhead failed. The well blew apart, triggering an explosion of flammable gases that claimed the lives of eleven innocent oil workers and caused billions of dollars in environmental damage. One witness in the congressional investigation called BP's failure to test the cement "horribly negligent."

In November 2012, the U.S. government banned BP from new federal contracts citing its "lack of business integrity" – an unwanted distinction that will likely tarnish BP's reputation for years to come.

Case Study – Catholic Church Scandal

The second example is the sexual abuse scandal involving a small percentage of Catholic priests that lead to numerous multi-million-dollar settlements. The severity of the scandal was amplified by the actions of certain church leaders who chose a cover-up

---

[3] Letter from U.S. Congress, House Committee on Energy and Commerce to Mr. Tony Hayward, CEO, BP PLC, June 14,2010

strategy in dealing with the crisis. There is evidence that, in some cases, the offenders were transferred from parish to parish instead of being denounced and reported to the authorities. In June 2012, Monsignor William J. Lynn of the archdiocese of Philadelphia was the first official to be convicted for his role in covering up sexual abuse by priests in his diocese.

The root cause of this tragic scandal is an extreme betrayal of trust perpetrated by debased individuals who committed the initial acts. However, once the evil perpetrators were discovered, the cover-up by some senior church leaders was most perplexing. The decision to not denounce and report offenders to the authorities is a leadership failure that the faithful congregation of the Catholic Church cannot tolerate.

Due to the injury caused to the church's reputation by the poor decisions of a few leaders, the circle of victims was enlarged from the unfortunate abused children to the entire community of Catholics and those the church serves. The congregation must demand greater accountability from its leaders when handling any crisis in the future. The church belongs to the congregation as much is it does to those who lead it.

No amount of leadership training can guarantee that an initial evil deed will be prevented. Leaders cannot possibly control the personal behavior of all their subordinates. However, how leaders react once they discover bad behavior is most certainly and entirely within their control. This is the important leadership lesson we can extract from this tragedy. Compounding wrongdoing by covering up the initial act is never an effective leadership strategy.

Virtues Help Avert Disasters

Most failures in leadership are preventable. If only the leaders involved practiced adherence to virtues, damage could in many cases be greatly contained. Think about how often you've seen similarly poor leadership behavior patterns in the organizations for which you've worked. Have you ever seen a leader hide bad news from superiors or shareholders? The damage and toll on humanity in the Gulf oil spill disaster and the aforementioned sex abuse scandal are extreme by comparison to common leadership failures in most organizations. However, the behavior pattern for many leadership failures is the same as the leadership failures discussed in the examples. *Strong adherence to well-developed virtues is the investment that companies can make to avoid compounding problems.* Interestingly, after the Gulf oil spill, BP revamped its corporate values to include an important virtue – courage. They now emphasize the importance of courage in speaking up and alerting superiors when dangerous decisions are being implemented.

It's important to acknowledge that there are thousands of leaders across societies all over the world who do the right thing nearly every day. We should celebrate their efforts. I also don't believe that by simply writing a leadership book stressing virtues, leaders will not make bad decisions anymore. Unfortunately, life doesn't work that way. However, virtues only emerge in an organization if they are taught, practiced, and reinforced consistently. The prevailing leadership culture across all organizations could use a good revival of virtue as a way of life. When faced with difficult circumstances resulting from the wrongdoing of others, well-trained leaders may then more easily determine what the appropriate response must be.

The Leadership Paradox

The paradox we face is that individuals who are frequently drawn to leadership positions are attracted by the love of power and money. We see this across the globe in dictatorships and in democracies where elected officials will do and say anything to hold on to their public office. This love of power is the wrong moral center and leads to eventual and inevitable failures of leadership. What we need in America and across the world is for leaders who hold a love of virtue as their moral center to rise up and take charge. The lovers of power create catastrophes; the lovers of virtue fix them. Nothing illustrates this point better than the emergence of Abraham Lincoln during the months leading up to the American Civil War.

As America's darkest hours approached during the early months of 1860, it almost seemed as if the hand of divine providence gave us Abraham Lincoln to confront the challenges of a fractured nation driven by the evil of slavery. With his election as president in November 1860, the nation went on to survive its gravest crisis. Here are two quotes from Mr. Lincoln that should serve as a guide for personal virtue in leadership:

> *"I am not bound to win, but I am bound to be true. I am not bound to succeed, but I am bound to live by the light that I have. I must stand with anybody that stands right, and stand with him while he is right, and part with him when he goes wrong."*

> *"Let's have faith that right makes might; and in that faith let us, to the end, dare to do our duty as we understand it."*

From where will the next Lincoln emerge? Can we make a commitment to lead like Lincoln in our everyday lives regardless of what level of leadership we occupy? Examine your moral center. If you have a love of virtue, by all means, answer the call of leadership.

4 Power Thoughts

1. What do you believe in?
2. Do you live by a moral code?
3. Have you examined the source of your moral code?
4. Are your beliefs compatible with a constructive leadership approach?
5. If you don't have a personal moral code, how do you expect to lead?

CHAPTER 7

Journey to the Center of You

"The most difficult thing in life is to know yourself."

– Thales

I n the preceding chapter, I explored the subject of introspection in the context of assessing your own moral center
in preparation for leadership. While the moral center is the bedrock of leadership, there is much more that a leader must understand about himself to maximize his effectiveness. There are many
tools available to assist with the process of self-discovery and introspection. I recommend tools in three broad categories – Personality Type Assessment, Emotional Assessment, and Multi-
Source Assessment.

Personality Type Assessment

Two popular personality type assessment tools have been in existence for quite some time. The first tool is the Myers-Briggs
Type Index (MBTI®). The tool was developed by Katharine
Cook-Briggs and her daughter, Isabel Briggs-Myers, based on the
writings and research of famed psychiatrist Carl Jung. The purpose of the tool is to determine how individuals perceive the
world and make decisions. The MBTI measures four sets of characteristics each with two possible preferences resulting in sixteen
distinct personality types. No single personality type is right or

wrong, but MBTI does identify strengths and weaknesses for each type.

Another very useful tool in understanding behavioral preferences and emotions is the DiSC® profile. The DiSC profile is based on the behavior model developed by Dr. William Marston and measures four behavioral dimensions – Dominance, Influence, Steadiness, and Compliance. According to Dr. Marston, "All people exhibit all four behavioral factors in varying degrees of intensity." The DiSC profile is useful in identifying a person's more pronounced tendencies. DiSC provides critical knowledge for a leader. It can provide an approach to identifying complementary personality types that can be used to counterbalance the leader's natural tendencies, thereby creating well-rounded teams. Further, DiSC assists teams in learning how to communicate more effectively with each other by highlighting preferred communication styles and needs.

It must be noted that both MBTI and DiSC identify preferred behaviors. They don't take into account intelligence, experience, training, values, or specific skills. This means that, through self-knowledge, the well-balanced leader can consciously choose a different behavior at any time. For example, someone who is naturally a risk taker may learn to exercise caution. Another leader who hates details may learn the value of examining details more often. Knowing how you're wired and how to complement your abilities is absolutely crucial in your leadership development process. These tests can provide invaluable insights into your abilities.

Furthermore, knowledge of diverse personality types and behaviors will help you to embrace and leverage differences in the personalities and qualities of others. The truly effective leader understands his own strengths and weaknesses, and he seeks to surround himself with people who complement them.

After doing or saying something based on an unfiltered reaction, have you ever wondered, "Why did I do that?" or "Where did that come from?" The MBTI and DiSC profiles can certainly help you answer these questions, but there is more to introspection than personality typing. To truly know yourself, you must have the courage to dig deeper for a more developed understanding of what drives your behavior.

Emotional Assessment

Often, deep-seeded effects of events and conditions that have shaped our lives also unconsciously drive our actions. These events and conditions can certainly be positive. For example, if as children we received constant positive affirmations regarding our self-worth and ability, we are influenced to become optimistic achievers. Conversely, we can also experience negative events and conditions that hold us back. These negative effects need to be identified and dealt with, or they can prevent a leader from achieving the proper balance needed to maintain effective relationships with others. Additionally, our positive nature must also be understood so it can be exploited to the greatest effect. I am recommending two tools for emotional assessment.

The first is very simple. It is the 4 Power Leadership Emotions Inventory. The Emotions Inventory is a categorized list of emotions. The list can be found as a free resource when you log into my website at www.4PowerLeadership.com. The Emotions Inventory is easy to use. Simply read through each listed emotion while preceding each listed emotion with the question, "I often feel..." Circle each emotion that you confirm as a frequent occurrence. Once you're done circling emotions, simply think back to all the times in your life where the circled emotions were most intense. What is the first time in your life that you can recall when you experienced a specific troubling emotion? What events stand out as potential sources of your most persistent emotions? After you've identified the sources of the negative emotions you carry, you can then begin to minimize their influence on your present life by learning to let go or manage these emotions more effectively.

The techniques for managing your emotions are provided by implementing the management strategies delineated in many books on Neuro-Linguistic Programming or in the many tools available in the field of Emotional Intelligence (EI). This brings me to my next recommended tool – an emotional intelligence inventory. There is actually a collection of tools that are classified as emotional intelligence inventories. A robust list can be found at www.eiconsortium.org.

Emotional Intelligence, as a field of study, dates back to the mid-1980s. The most prominent names in the field are a pair of researchers, Peter Salovey and John D. Mayer, who published a pioneering article in 1990. Their theory is based on the premise that people possess emotional intelligence in addition to cognitive intelligence. Emotional intelligence is defined as the ability to accurately assess, express, and regulate emotion in oneself and others. It defines a framework based on four factors: self-awareness, self-management, social awareness, and relationship management. Emotional intelligence inventories and assessments can be completed online at various sites or by participating in a facilitated session with a certified professional.

Multi-Source Assessment

The last tool I recommend is valuable in self-assessment because it provides constructive feedback on how others view us. It is the multi-rater feedback survey or 360° feedback survey. The

Emotional and Social Competence Inventory is an EI assessment tool that is also a 360° survey. This survey collects feedback from peers, subordinates, and superiors with whom a specific leader routinely interacts. The responses received are then compared to the leader's answers. The survey is designed to help the leader learn how other people see him or her in comparison to one's own opinion. The results are sometimes stunning eye-openers and can be very useful in highlighting areas for leader development.

Look Inside Objectively

Looking within yourself with unvarnished objectivity can be very unsettling. It requires great courage and a deep commitment to introspection and self-analysis. At this point, I must caution readers. If you feel you have a serious problem in your past, I encourage you to seek out professional help because deep introspection can take you to some dark places. Some of you can manage these dark places, and as you identify them, you can "clean out the closet." Once your persistent negative emotions are identified, you can then make adjustments in your behavior to minimize their effects. However, people dealing with deeper emotional problems may require the assistance of a trained professional.

Some of you may be surprised that I'm discussing advice on emotional healing in a leadership book. After all, why would a leader have any emotional problems? Aren't leaders strong people who don't have internal issues? Aren't emotional issues found only in weaker people? There are only two kinds of people – those who are wounded and those who are lying about it! People can be compulsively and unconsciously driven by internal qualities that shaped them throughout the course of their lives. Leaders cannot afford to operate without full knowledge of what drives them internally.

Some of your more unsavory qualities are often rooted in the events that shaped you years ago. We all have emotional baggage, so you need to confront it, pack it, and dump it. Why is this important? You can't lead effectively if your hurts are leading you. Become the "captain of your soul." Leaders whose inner emotions are dominated by past events are not fully in control of themselves. Therefore, it's hard to achieve the poise that a leader must have to maximize effectiveness.

You must come to a realization and acceptance that the past cannot be changed. Whether you're dealing with a wrong someone did to you or a serious mistake you made, letting go is your most powerful weapon. Fighting the past is like trying to fight a ghost. If we all knew then what we know now, we would all do things differently. The past can only serve as a teacher for future behavior.

Letting go of the past by forgiving yourself and others who have wronged you is the only viable option. The alternative is misery and an ever-increasing load of baggage. Just choose to drop the baggage. Once you do, the result is liberation achieved by knowing that what was weighing you down no longer has any effect on you. For the routine difficulties people encounter in life, it's really that simple. However, it may take time to come to the realization that you can liberate yourself whenever you choose.

Your Baggage is a Choice

What about people who have suffered serious tragedies? Can they ever be liberated from the emotional weight of their trauma? The answer is yes. The resilient people able to confront tragedy and restore their positive outlooks are truly special and are all the more inspirational to us all. If someone can overcome tragedy and still maintain a positive outlook, our troubles can seem small by comparison. There are remarkable people in this world who realize that they have a choice to either overcome their tragedies or let the tragedies define them for the rest of their lives. Some are even able to turn their tragedy into a source of strength.

I've had the distinct honor to meet and converse with several wounded warriors who have suffered horrific injuries in the recent Iraq and Afghanistan Wars. I am always so deeply impressed by the resilience of their spirit. Many of them take on leadership roles doing charitable work to help their fellow wounded warriors. It was this personal experience with these heroes that caused me to be particularly moved and fascinated by the story of J.R. Martinez.[4] I became aware of J.R. Martinez when I watched him on the popular TV show *Dancing with the Stars*. His story inspired me and led me to do further research on his life and the circumstances of his injuries.

He grew up mostly in Arkansas until the age of 18 when he and his mother moved to Dalton, Georgia. In Dalton, J.R. enjoyed playing strong safety on the high school football team. He was a very popular young man and a leader. He'd always dreamed of playing professional football, but those dreams faded quickly due to injury and grades that didn't quite meet NCAA standards.

Looking for fresh alternatives, J.R. went to see a recruiter after viewing a TV commercial about the Army. J.R. decided to enlist. He traveled to Ft. Benning, Georgia where he attended basic training and received his advanced individual training as an infantryman. By January 2003, J.R. went on to Fort Campbell, Kentucky where he was assigned to the famed 101st Airborne Division. In March of that same year, J.R. deployed to Iraq.

On April 5, 2003, J.R. and his platoon were on a mission traveling on a dusty desert road heading north from the city of Kar-

---

[4] J.R. Martinez' story is used with his permission.

bala, Iraq, located about 62 miles southwest of Baghdad. J.R. was serving as the driver of a Humvee that also carried three of his fellow soldiers. Suddenly, the left front tire of his Humvee struck a land mine. The three passengers escaped with minor injuries, but J.R. was trapped inside. The instant he heard the blast, he felt an intense flash of heat come up through the floorboard. Less than a month into his tour, J.R. had sustained burns over 34 percent of his body, and he was thrust into a fight for survival. J.R. was quickly evacuated to a local medic station and then rapidly on to Germany for initial treatment. He was then sent to Brook Army Medical Center in San Antonio, Texas where he would spend the next 34 months in recovery and undergo 33 different surgeries.

During his time in recovery, he was asked to speak to another burn patient who was in a deep state of depression. After a 45-minute visit, the patient's outlook took a positive turn. Before meeting with J.R., he kept his room dark and closed. After the meeting, the patient finally opened the curtain to his room, letting daylight into his life. Through this event and sharing his story with others, J.R. began to understand the inspirational impact he could have on people's lives. Slowly his calling in life would become clear. J.R. became a motivational speaker and today has a thriving career. He even landed a role on a daytime soap opera. J.R. has an irrepressible smile and a personality that makes you look completely past his scars. But J.R.'s story gets even better.

As I mentioned at the start of J.R.'s story, he was a contestant on *Dancing with the Stars*. J.R. not only had 10 weeks of fun dancing with his lovely professional dance partner, but he actually won the competition! J.R. clearly does not let adversity hold him back. Learn more about him at *www.jrmartinez.com* and in his book, *Full of Heart: My Story of Survival, Strength, and Spirit.*

Connect with the Greater You

Positive leaders understand themselves, and have harnessed the qualities and events that shape their personality, both good and bad. I'm challenging you to figure out what makes you tick. It's my firm belief that if you have this answer, you'll be a better leader.

Once you've liberated yourself from the things that weigh you down, the next step is to overcome the fear of embracing the creative qualities within you. Doing so allows you to connect with your true calling and become the fullest expression of the person you were meant to become. It is surprisingly common for this step in the journey of self-discovery to generate some anxiety. Once discovered, your calling demands accountability. You have to act on your calling or you won't be completely happy. It is our human mission to put more into the earth than we take out. That is a life of fulfillment. That's the life of a leader.

4 Power Thoughts

1. Do you think you have the courage for deep introspection?
   a. What significant events in your life shaped your personality the most?
2. What can you do to compensate for your undesirable behavioral traits?
   a. Do you know the root cause of these traits?
3. What personality traits should you seek out in subordinates that will complement your personality and emerging leadership style?
   a. Identify at least one personality trait in you that would require a complementary personality to enhance your effectiveness?

CHAPTER 8

Roadblocks to Poise

"Self-reverence, self-knowledge, self-control; these three alone lead one to sovereign power."

— *Alfred Lord Tennyson*

A s you endeavor to establish a poised leadership core, you will most likely encounter potential traps that can threaten your development into a poised and effective leader. In this chapter, you'll learn about ways to avoid these snares.

Anger

Anger isn't always inappropriate. It's sometimes justified, particularly in cases when you're in physical danger. Anger is also appropriate when you're expressing righteous indignation. However, anger often has powerful strings that stretch back to events in your past. Because of these powerful connections, when you're in certain situations, anger can become an out-of-control, disproportionate response to the present situation. When your reaction is overblown, you're more likely reacting to events in the past that you haven't resolved. Without realizing it, you may be reaching back to past feelings, pulling them forward, and attaching those feelings to the present situation. For example, if you suffered injustice in childhood, you may develop an acute sensitivity to any hint of injustice. Or, if you were ridiculed as a child, you may carry a deep sense of insecurity into adulthood that may cause you to be hypersensitive when challenged by subordinates.

Anger is a secondary emotion, meaning that when you're angry, there is something else that is at the root of your anger. Disappointment in love is certainly one possibility. Anger can also be a manifestation of fear or frustration. If you become overly anxious regarding the outcome of a project or task, an outburst of anger may result when obstacles are encountered. The outburst of anger is likely rooted in your fear of failure and the possibility of failure leading to ridicule.

For some of you, simply being aware of the connection of anger to your formative years can be enough to help you control and channel this emotion effectively. Dealing with your anger is another reason to engage in the introspective analysis recommended in Chapter 7.

Many behavior patterns can be said to have an attachment to your childhood. Why single out anger? In the context of leadership, uncontrolled anger is the surest way to lose your followers. The loss of respect for a leader who succumbs to uncontrolled fits of anger is profound. I remember an incident quite clearly that occurred when I was working as a project manager for a small information technology company.

One day, our CEO discovered $450 in charges on the company phone bill as the result of calls someone made to a porn line. The CEO assembled all the employees into his rather large and ostentatious office. He then delivered a profanity-laced tirade against the unidentified perpetrator. The CEO never uttered a single word to assuage the feelings of the innocents who were also bearing the brunt of his anger. Being one of the innocent, I didn't feel accused or responsible in the least, but I completely lost respect for that CEO. I felt insulted. Watching him yell with his veins bulging in his forehead gave me a clear sense that I was working for the wrong man. Subjecting all his employees to this unnecessary spectacle succeeded only in demonstrating how little he respected his employees. Having lost respect for him, I immediately began searching for a new job. I knew I could no longer work for that CEO.

The damage that this sort of behavior does to an organization would be simple to measure if the only impact were departing employees. However, the total loss of inspiration among those who remain is widespread and chronic. The employees who stay behind begin to perform at minimally acceptable levels – just enough to retain their jobs. If a leader's primary role is to inspire, the undesirable effect of a tirade is the very manifestation of "anti-leadership."

The proper response for this CEO would have been to appropriately channel his righteous anger by explaining the damage that the individual was doing to the company and soliciting everyone's help in identifying the culprit. Better yet, the CEO could have said nothing. He could have analyzed data from the office phone system and worked to identify the culprit. Instead, his loss of control forfeited all such opportunities for investigation, insulted the innocent, and demoralized his workforce in one thoughtless act.

The typical leader is also particularly vulnerable to anger resulting from simple frustration generated by the normal everyday execution of his duties. Leading people takes enormous patience and tolerance for mistakes and misunderstanding.

Loss of patience because of frustration and expression of the resulting anger in an uncontrolled manner will demoralize subordinates as quickly as the profanity-slinging CEO. Justifiable anger arising from normal dealings with subordinates must be rechanneled properly into effective communication and need not be expressed as anger at all. When you begin to feel frustrated, you must push your listening skills into overdrive. You must truly try to understand the root of the problem you're facing. Questioning intended to gain full understanding can open doors in relationships by demonstrating that you have an active interest in the problem at hand and are invested in your subordinate's success. The effective leader must be a fountain of patience in the presence of subordinates even when their behavior is perplexing.

Restraint Defeats Frustration

The consistent demonstration of personal restraint in difficult situations will serve to enhance trust and your subordinates' perception of you as an approachable leader. When I've been able to demonstrate great restraint in difficult circumstances, the results have been extraordinary. I was complimented on my obvious show of restraint, and it also enhanced my stature as a leader.

However, your patience in dealing with subordinate foul-ups also doesn't mean that you must accept the almost infinite variety of excuses that subordinates often invent. You can let subordinates know they are on an unacceptable course without getting angry. You can be firm and clear in a controlled manner without a single blood vessel bulging from your forehead. Ultimately, if the same problem persists, you have to decide whether the cause is a personnel problem or whether there is some other cause such as a systemic or interdepartmental disconnect.

One of my "favorite" leadership frustrations is a subordinate's lack of initiative in dealing with obstacles. I've often handed a project or task to a subordinate and checked on progress at some later point only to discover that very little had been accomplished. In other cases, I've had subordinates who were unstoppable. The difference is often in their approach to obstacles. The person who stops at the first encounter with difficulty either lacks initiative, has weak communication skills, or is reticent in confronting the source of resistance.

You cannot let your frustration lead to an outburst of anger when subordinates repeatedly fail to surmount obstacles. A measured response to an unmet expectation can be expressed with restrained tones. Describe what you desire in crystal clear terms while soliciting understanding and confirmation from your subordinate. Actively listen to determine the cause of the obstacle. Your role is to coach the employee to success. If necessary and appropriate, remove the obstacle for them. Better still, help them talk through a solution with you so next time they can remove the obstacle on their own. As a last resort, remove the subordinate from the task if the behavior pattern is consistently not improved. Some people are just excuse factories. You won't be able to fix them. Cut your losses and move on. However, if you break down in anger, your lack of poise will cause you to lose the whole team.

Lack of focus on common goals is another source of frustration I've often encountered over the course of my career. A highly dysfunctional organization that is mired in interdepartmental rivalries can easily degrade into self-defeating behavior and lose sight of their mission.

During my Army career, a few uncooperative government civilian employees who were constantly in a defensive political posture, particularly challenged my patience. These troublesome few were more concerned with not being blamed for failure than creating success. It became a personal challenge to defeat the obstacles their departments presented. Since I didn't have the authority to directly confront and correct the causes of the rivalries, I often circumvented them. I used creative processes, coalitions of the willing, and personal initiative in completing work for which they were technically responsible.

In corporate life, I've often had more direct control in solving organizational dysfunction. Corporations have a built-in incentive to resolve organizational dysfunction. If they don't, they'll be out of business. In situations where elements of my team were not working cooperatively, I corrected the problem by stressing teamwork and making process adjustments that reduced friction. However, I also made it clear that if everyone didn't start pulling in the same direction, personnel changes would ensue.

Don't Fight the System – Fix it!

Bureaucracy and difficult processes can be a further source of frustration. Some leaders just rail against the system. Their outbursts only serve to diminish their image in the eyes of subordinates. Other leaders gain prestige by changing the processes or mastering them to their own advantage.

When correcting a process is not feasible, my short-term approach is to master a difficult process and work toward perfection within it. If you do this, there is no possibility of your actions or requests being rejected. The people who run the process will appreciate you because you're demonstrating how seriously you respect their system. In the future, they'll be more forgiving and helpful when you hit a snag. The last thing you want to do is rail in anger at some unfortunate subordinate who is merely trying to get by with the poorly designed process he or she's been handed. I've seen managers take this approach, and they only succeeded in destroying their own image.

Correcting ineffective processes is one of my favorite strategies. Casting yourself as a crusader against inefficiency can significantly enhance your leadership image as a problem solver. People hate drudgery, and when they are powerless to change it, their spirit sinks. Enter a leader who is determined to defeat drudgery by implementing streamlined processes, and he will be hailed as a deliverer of the downtrodden. Succumb to anger from frustration, and you are reduced to a small and pathetic caricature.

Once I encountered a situation where my employer was incapable of producing a timely and accurate invoice for a computer desktop outsourcing contract we held with the federal government. The customer's frustrations were skyrocketing because he didn't trust us anymore. If we were incapable of producing a bill, how could we be trusted to run their computer systems? Our employee morale was at an extreme low because they knew the customer did not respect us.

Also, employees hate the idea that their employer is not being compensated for their labor, even if they are still drawing paychecks despite the company's inability to collect. After all, getting paid is the ultimate objective and measure of success in business. The awful invoicing situation weighed on everyone. The employees knew we were losing money like a leaky dam. It was depressing, but many became conditioned to accept the poor state of affairs because they felt powerless to change the system.

I had a different perspective. I believed that all it took was some focused planning and determination to not accept the status quo. I methodically picked the current system apart. I figured out what the billing requirements were and developed an extremely detailed specification that I handed off to a programmer. Within 60 days, we had implemented a replacement system that shortened our invoicing cycle from an average of two and half months to just three days! Ineffective managers wallow in their self-reinforcing defeatism caused by what they often misperceive as hopeless circumstances. Whenever possible, don't get angry. Instead, grab the bull by the horns and change the system. That's what leaders do.

When dealing with bureaucracy, always remember one thing – bureaucracies are composed of people. Dealing with people is where true leaders shine. Never approach a bureaucratic obstacle by just throwing your request into the "system" and hoping for the best. Make strong personal connections with key people across the organization. Nurture these relationships so you always have a contact to solve problems and expedite solutions. But no matter what, never relinquish your self-control. Anger is useless.

Fear

Life presents opportunities. Leaders must be ready to accept and exploit these opportunities. Look for the open doors. Expect them. When they open, do not hesitate to run through them. Fear determines whether we run through the open door or lose the opportunity. Abigail Adams used these words to inspire her husband John in the pursuit of independence for the American colonies:

> *"There is a tide in the affairs of men.*
> *Which, taken at the flood, leads on to fortune;*
> *Omitted, all the voyage of their life*
> *Is bound in shallows and in miseries.*
> *On such a full sea are we now afloat,*
> *And we must take the current when it serves,*
> *Or lose our ventures."*
>
> *–Shakespeare ("Julius Caesar")*

Subordinates respect leaders who can exercise prudent boldness. This comes from a combination of desire for achievement while feeling safe in the process. The leader who demonstrates fear erodes confidence the latter being the most prominent trait that subordinates look for in a leader. When the leader allows fear to erode confidence, defections among subordinates are sure to follow.

Fear is the great immobilizer and thief of dreams. Unless conquered, the only fruits of fear are bitterness and regret over ventures not attempted. Fear takes on many forms:

- *Fear of failure* – To a leader, the potential for ridicule and loss of prestige can lead to an overabundance of caution.
- *Fear of criticism* – If you were to try to solve world hunger, you would still have critics. Criticism should be expected and anticipated when leading.
- *Fear of the unknown* – Leaders are constantly facing straight into the unknown. Dealing with the unknown is at the core of leadership. You must be comfortable with venturing forward. It's the whole point of being a leader.
- *Fear of change* – This fear can be a leader's undoing if he refuses to accept that circumstances of his position or strategy have changed and he fails to adapt.
- *Fear of the inner demons* – Your nasty inner demons must be slain so they don't pop out and inject fear when you least expect it. That's why Chapter 7 is so important.

Generally, we all have fear, and if you don't feel it when fear is justified, something is wrong. The key is to not let fear overtake you to the point where you can't function effectively as a leader. Unless conquered, fear will churn like an excuse factory spewing mental obstacles 24x7. That is the net effect of unrestrained fear. The well-adjusted leader keeps fear under control. He uses it positively by allowing fear to keep him sharp. Fear is a catalyst for controlling risk to the greatest reasonable extent. We can become "fearless" when we have so subjugated this emotion that its effect on our leadership capability is negligible.

"A man is but the product of his thoughts – what he thinks, he becomes."

– Mohandas Gandhi

The best advice for overcoming fear is to first identify the form to which you are most susceptible. Trace back to the earliest recollections that triggered this fear. If you visit my website, www.4PowerLeadership.com, you can download the Emotions Inventory for free. This tool can be helpful in tracing the sources of all your negative emotions.

Once you have identified the fear, controlling your thoughts is essential to preventing the fear from overwhelming you. Identify one thing you could do that would lessen the fear and do it. Replace negative, anxiety-building thoughts with positive affirmations. There are techniques for this in the field of Neuro-Linguistic Programming that I have found very helpful in managing nearly all emotional states.

Last, deliberately place yourself in situations where you have to confront the fear to which you are most commonly susceptible. Push your personal comfort envelope. Over time you will strengthen your ability to control your fears. Fear never completely goes away, but you can definitely prevent being dominated by fearful thoughts.

Emotional Turbulence

Have you ever been around people who are so emotionally variable that you never know what to expect? One minute they're smiling, while the next minute they are sullen. One minute they're calm and patient. The next minute they are short tempered and biting people's heads off.

Emotional unpredictability is very unsettling to subordinates. They seek stability in their leader. They want to know that he or she is a steady source of strength and can be relied upon in times of crisis. It's important that the poised leader demonstrate calm under pressure. A cool head will allow you to think clearly and develop solutions.

Even when things are going well, the poised leader must remain restrained. Unrestrained euphoria during success is as dangerous as depression during difficulty. Never allow yourself to get too high or too low. If you doubt that unrestrained euphoria is damaging to a leader's image, search YouTube for the infamous incident that was the undoing of Howard Dean's presidential campaign. After the Iowa caucuses for the 2004 Democratic primary election, Dean decided he would rally his troops by demonstrating high-energy enthusiasm over the progress his campaign was making. Unfortunately, he let his enthusiasm get away from him, and he delivered a "primal scream" in the course of his rallying speech. He thought he was energizing the crowd, but instead, the long-term result was a huge loss of respect from his support base. He became cannon fodder for the late night comedians. David Letterman delivered this stinging quip:

> *"Here's what happened: The people of Iowa realized they didn't want a president with the personality of a hockey dad."*

No one respects someone who is out of control.

Lack of Self-discipline

The leader is the spark plug that fires the organizational engine. If you lack the self-discipline to follow through on actions or develop a reputation for not doing what you say you're going to do, then the organization you lead will quickly become rudder-less. Your subordinates will ignore your requests and directives because they will quickly realize that your interest in your requests will not be sustained. In effect, you've conditioned them to ex-hibit this response by your lack of follow through. People only pay attention to what you perceive is important. When you don't follow through, you're telling them that what you said was not important. They are following your lead!

Self-discipline can be nurtured by developing good habits. First, be committed to following through on personal actions. If you say you're going to do something first thing in the morning, then do it. This is a simple commitment you can make to yourself for everyday tasks. It will teach you personal accountability.

Second, pick a longer-term personal or work goal. Define the goal clearly with a specific desired outcome. Setting a goal crys-tallizes what you want and helps you to visualize the result. Next, make a list of the steps needed to achieve that goal with a defini-tive time frame for completing each step. Keep your plan where you can see it every day, and check off the steps as you complete them. This tactic of personal goal-setting will help nurture good habits of tracking your activities. It will also give you great satis-faction as you see progress against your goal. Clear all distractions and do what needs to be done with minimal procrastination.

Maintaining a personal regimen of sufficient sleep, healthy diet, and regular exercise is also part of self-discipline, and helps to project your image as a serious person who has his own life un-der control. Would you trust a leader to control an organization when he can't control himself? Exercising self-restraint in what we eat and drink will not only give you the energy you need to succeed, but it will help you maintain your leadership image.

4 Power Thoughts

1. To which of the top threats to poise do you think you are most vulnerable?

    a. Do you have another vulnerability to poise not listed?

2. What goal would you like to set to help you nurture your self-discipline?

    a. What is your plan to achieve this goal?

3. Are you prone to anger?

    a. If yes, to what can you trace this feeling?

4. Do your emotional reactions remain balanced whether you're happy or sad?

CHAPTER 9

Poise Achieved

"There is no greater mastery than mastery of the self and its passions, for it amounts to the triumph of free will."

– Baltasar Gracián

D eveloping the Power of Poise requires completing the journey to the center of you. Achieving poise means that you have become the owner of your emotions and you have the confidence to accept who you are. The key is self-acceptance and showing that you are comfortable in your own skin. Self-acceptance doesn't mean that you should be satisfied with the state of all your emotional qualities. It simply means that you understand them and you no longer chastise yourself with negative internal "conversations." Full knowledge of who you are and what makes you the way you are places you in the driver's seat of your own life. You are no longer subject to knee-jerk reactions driven by emotions you don't understand. The poised leader understands his personal composition. This understanding leads to complete self-possession and ownership of your own psychology.

The achievement of poise means that any baggage you may have accumulated no longer controls you. Your strength is now derived from your inner sense of calm in knowing exactly who you are.

The poised leader has a deep inner commitment to virtue. The strong moral core further strengthens one's leadership ability through a belief that right creates might. The poised leader draws further calmness and inner peace in knowing that his actions are derived from a sound moral foundation. The virtue of courage is the antidote to normal fears arising from our daily encounters in everyday leadership situations. The poised leader is committed to advancing virtue as his leadership platform.

Having successfully completed the journey of introspection, you are now able to fully engage with others as a principled and well-balanced leader. How do you communicate the strength and confidence of the inner you to the external world? How do you ensure that you are perceived as the leader you are inside? How do you manage the image of the external you? The next power – the Power of Presence is the answer.

4 Power Thoughts

1. How would your outlook on life be different if you had a sense of total calm inside?
2. Use the 4 Power Leadership Emotions Inventory to examine the drivers behind your negative emotions. Visit the website at www.4PowerLeadership.com.
3. Consider working with a leadership coach to help you clarify your vision and more clearly define who you are as a leader.

Section 2
Presence

CHAPTER 10

Presence: The Second Power

"Remember that it is the actions, and not the commission, that make the officer, and that there is more expected from him, than the title."

– George Washington

P resence is all about projecting your image as a leader. A strong and positive leadership presence is the external manifestation of the poised inner you. People often struggle with "internal noise" driven by insecurities and a value system that is not balanced by virtues. This "noise" muddles the external expression of a confident image. Once you've established poise, the noise has been substantially reduced, if not eliminated entirely. Then, you're more likely to project positive leadership qualities as you interact with people around you.

You project an image of yourself to others whether you're aware of it or not. The Power of Presence is a purposeful, yet natural, projection of your confident inner leadership core compared to the unfiltered and raw projection of personality when you lack leadership poise. Think of a time when you first met a group of people from the same company or organization. Usually, you can identify the "power" in the group. This is because the individual with the power is often projecting his presence effec-

tively as the leader. You can just tell by the way the person behaves and carries himself that he is confident and in control. He is
rarely the most outspoken or the one directing traffic. Most
likely, he will be low-key in the way he introduces himself.

The poised leader is always aware of the image he is projecting. The stronger you are internally and the more settled you are
in your feelings and outlook, the stronger your leadership presence will be. Achieving inner poise is absolutely essential as the
foundation for projecting your leadership presence. Without
poise, your subordinates will begin to feel that something isn't
quite right about you. This perception will undermine their confidence in you. Your conflicted and unsettled character will create
disconnects between your body language and what you say. People subtly detect these incongruities in others all the time, even if
they can't quite put their finger on exactly why they don't feel
right about someone. If your subordinates constantly sense this
about you, your presence will be greatly diminished, and you will
find yourself leaning more heavily on autocratic or formal authority for leadership impact. Conversely, with a strongly poised inner
self, your external projections will be consistent and much more
apt to inspire confidence in others. With practice and further
learning, your presence can be enhanced. You can become that
individual with the power whom people pick out in a crowd.

Presence vs. Charisma

Leadership presence is not to be confused with charisma, although presence can have a charismatic effect. Over the course of
my career, I've met many very charismatic people who, although
irresistible on a personal level, were not necessarily effective leaders. In fact, many of these people relied on their charisma almost
exclusively to get by. Once you moved beyond their thin veneer,

you were left greatly disappointed in their lack of depth and substance. Their leadership presence evaporated, and they were reduced to mere charmers. Charm wears thin after a while, and the effects of pure charisma are fleeting. Presence is about substance and authenticity, but charisma is superficial.

This does not mean that charisma is unnecessary to be an effective leader. In fact, charisma combined with strong presence is the ideal external projection of the leadership image. Charisma, like all other leadership qualities, can be cultivated. In some cases, people who seem to naturally exude high levels of charisma also become effective leaders through study, commitment, and self-discipline. These types are indeed "dangerous." They have a powerful combination of qualities at work in their favor – the instant rapport of charisma and enduring leadership presence.

Sometimes someone can achieve great success in a specific circumstance and then build off that success to create a reputation and an aura of leadership. This situation requires continued functional area competence in order for a leader to be fully effective. Success in one area that is leveraged into leadership aura doesn't necessarily transfer competence to a new leadership situation. An aura of success contributes to a leader's presence but doesn't necessarily establish competence. Be wary of leaders that project presence through mere use of circumstantial aura. To illustrate this point, here's a useful example.

An executive had built a reputation for success by closing a major multi-million dollar computer hardware deal with a customer. The deal size was unprecedented in his corporation and provided a transformative infusion of revenue for his organization. The executive became very highly regarded with corporate management. He was then promoted to division president and given responsibility for multiple market segments, which now also included a significant consulting and information technology services practice. The dynamics of the hardware business and services business are significantly different and require diverse competencies.

The executive had built an "aura of success" from his reputation in hardware sales. He leaned heavily on this aura as the main component of his leadership presence. His "leadership by aura" was marginally effective because his core skills were somewhat diluted, having been thrust into a new market segment of which he had only limited knowledge. This resulted in several years of poor results during which the executive was never able to duplicate the success of the megadeal that had boosted his career. His dependence on aura alone was not enough for him to establish the leadership presence required for sustained success. That's why you need to build your aura through a genuine leadership presence that flows from your character, personal traits, and competence. Your subordinates will then view you as an authentic leader, not a flash in the pan. Now, let's examine the relationship of leadership presence to organizational culture.

Presence Defines Culture

As the leader, you are the heartbeat of your organization's culture. Without strong leadership presence, your organization's culture will define itself into some low-performing state in which no one is happy. The culture of any organization mirrors the character of the man or woman at the top. If the leader is driven, focused, and results oriented, his organization will exhibit the same characteristics. If the leader takes prudent risks, is not afraid to fail, and displays the confidence to course correct, then his organization will be more entrepreneurial and aggressive. In contrast, if the leader is reticent and vacillates at the first sign of difficulty, has trouble sticking to a plan, and doesn't accept sound advice when course corrections are in order, then the organization will take on a passive wait-and-see culture. Even worse, if the leader displays a habit of punishing failure, he'll soon be making all the decisions himself because none of his subordinates will want to take any risks.

A reward of leadership is the opportunity to put your stamp on an organization as you work toward the attainment of common goals. For better or worse, intentionally or unintentionally, the personality of the leader is injected into all levels of the organization. That's why you should develop a conscious plan to infuse your team with the desired positive culture. As the leader, you must work tirelessly to project your core vision downward and across your entire organization through consistent and frequent communication. When your team starts to echo back your vision through their feedback and actions, you know you've succeeded in establishing your presence.

Presence and Perception

The next leadership question to consider is, "Are you tall enough to lead?" This question has nothing to do with your physical height. In fact, Napoleon can serve as an example for invalidating any perception that physical height is restrictive in one's ability to lead. Depending on whom you believe, Napoleon was either 5 feet 2 inches or 5 feet 6 inches. (There is some controversy surrounding whether the British or French measurement systems were used to record his height.) Regardless of his actual height, Napoleon's reputation remains intact throughout recorded history – a diminutive man who was a giant as a leader.

To counter his physical appearance, Napoleon always remained keenly aware of the image he was projecting at all times. Being a master speaker, Napoleon knew how to enlarge his psychological presence to overcome his diminutive stature. In his book, *Speak Like Churchill, Stand Like Lincoln,* James C. Humes described Napoleon's use of the "Power Pause." Prior to beginning speeches to rally his troops, he would create a tension that made him seem powerful and in command. This technique enhanced his stature and helped him cast his presence among his armies. After experiencing one of his speeches, Napoleon's troops must have imagined him a giant. As Herold said, in his book, *The Age of Napoleon:*

> *"Napoleon was the kind of man who could make himself obeyed with one glance of his cold gray eyes."*

By asking, "Are you tall enough to lead?" I mean, are you perceived by subordinates as having sufficient stature to function as their leader? Will subordinates perceive you as someone to whom they can commit? Your stature is established by developing your Power of Presence.

Your presence must also fit your role. If you're leading a small team of accounts receivables clerks, you don't act like you're the CEO. Conversely, if you are the CEO, you can't be chasing details like a low-level clerk. You have to grow into the role you occupy and project a presence that reinforces the image that people expect of someone in that role. Your behavior must synchronize with the part.

Presence and Authority

Presence also has a clear link to authority. Developing a keen understanding of authority and its use in establishing your leadership presence is also a skill to be mastered for developing your presence. There are three types of authority – official authority, implied authority, and perceived authority. *Official authority* is the detailed written company description of your assignment. It's your written charter defining the level of formal power you have within an organization. *Implied authority* is the extension of your official authority by virtue of logical extrapolations that are generally accepted by the organization at large. Implied authority isn't necessarily written down in formal descriptions. Last, and most importantly, is *perceived authority*. Perceived authority can be much higher or much lower than official authority depending on how well you've projected your leadership presence.

A very senior executive may have a high degree of official authority, but his perceived authority may be low among his subordinates because the executive is not respected and is somehow perceived as weak. Conversely, there are cases when people with low official authority actually wield great power, because they are highly respected leaders within the informal organization and no one makes a move without their consent. Because of the respect they garner, the organization perceives them to have much greater authority than they are officially apportioned.

Perceived authority can be enhanced through two primary methods – extraordinary expertise and influence. Generally, throughout my career, I've tended to achieve higher perceived authority than my official authority. I've achieved high perceived authority by being thoroughly knowledgeable in my job function and exercising influence through persuasion and logical arguments. Through these techniques, you can consistently influence the direction of organizations, even when your official authority is low.

Growing Your Presence

How do you grow your presence? We already looked at how the beginning of presence is generated by what you carry inside you. As you project the strength of your inner character, people will begin to see you differently. Your confidence and strength become contagious.

The next step in nurturing your Power of Presence is leveraging the tool of association by establishing strong linkages between you, unassailable values, and grand goal-oriented themes. The grand themes and visions you advance must resonate with the core of every person in your organization. You will want to start associating yourself with larger ideals. For example, associate yourself with the idea of achieving a grand organizational goal, high integrity, or high quality results. These are all lofty inspirational themes that are greater than any one single individual. When people believe that you and these lofty visions are one and the same, your presence is elevated and magnified. The associations you make must be genuine. If they are contrived and you don't believe them yourself, your charade will be discovered in due course and your image will collapse permanently. Again, honesty is the cornerstone of leadership.

The leader who wants to establish the strongest possible positive presence should promote alignment and association with strong common values and principles. Your relationships begin to fall into place as you positively influence those around you to gravitate toward those higher ideals. You must be uncompromising in adherence to the high road. You must stick to your principles like hugging a pillar in a storm because you will certainly be tested. If you promote high values and principles and then abandon or compromise them at the first encounter with difficulty, then your leadership credentials will be vaporized along with your presence. Your demonstrated will in standing for what is right serves to cement your presence as a leader.

Some people try to extend their presence by associating themselves closely with a respected or powerful superior. For example,

PRESENCE: THE SECOND POWER • 99

if the leader over you is highly respected and people know that his confidence and authority is vested in you, then your association with that leader will extend your presence to a degree. In the short run, this can be very effective, but the technique has a downside. Some may actually interpret your association with the superior as weakness if you make it appear that your only source of presence depends on your relationship with your superior. Additionally, your close association creates a dependency for your leadership presence that can ultimately work against you if the leader you associate with falls out of favor. Close association with a superior leader is different than having access. Simple access can extend your perceived authority, thereby boosting your presence. However, close association should be considered with great care because of the downside that all of your superior's sins will be viewed as your own if performance turns negative.

Presence Ignites Confidence

By now, the connection between the poised inner self and the ability to establish your leadership presence should be clear. What you feel and believe inside comes through to the outside. The more you manifest the positive qualities embraced by the inner self, the stronger and more unassailable your leadership position becomes, thereby projecting the leadership presence needed to win over your subordinates.

Presence is probably the most difficult of the 4 Powers to master. Presence is the power that ignites confidence in one's subordinates. The coming chapters will give you the key tools that you need to cultivate your Power of Presence. Your challenge is to learn how to use these tools and put them to work for you. The first tool is easy to master. It is also free and you probably already use it every day.

4 Power Thoughts

1. Who do you know that has a strong leadership presence?
   a. What quality about that individual makes you feel that he or she is a leader?
2. Do you feel confident when you're in a leadership position?
   a. Why or why not?

CHAPTER 11

Do You Know that Your Greatest Asset is Free?

"Sometimes your joy is the source of your smile, but sometimes your smile can be the source of your joy."

– *Thich Nhat Hanh*

Your best asset is your smile. Your smile is a powerful tool for self-actualization. Smiling raises your energy level. The positive frame of mind created by maintaining a smile positions you to look for opportunities and positive outcomes. The smile settles the soul and positions your mind to expect success.

Your effectiveness is reduced if you're constantly sullen and frowning. When you have a negative frame of mind and people see a gloomy look on your face, they can only deduce that things are not well. Worse yet, they don't know why, and their imaginations will start to fill in the blanks.

Conversely, it's very difficult to smile and think negative thoughts at the same time. Maintaining your smile in spite of encountering routine obstacles and difficulties helps to keep these negative thoughts in check. You really do have far more reasons to smile than you think. Your smile helps you manage your troubles. In your leadership role, always do your best to manage a smile. No one appreciates a leader who constantly wears his frustrations on his sleeve. Wear your smile instead.

Your Smile Builds Your Charisma

Have you ever noticed that magnetic people seem to have an aura about them? If you examine their demeanor, you'll find that they are usually smiling. They seem to glitter. People want to be around happy people. If you want to draw people to you, you've got to smile!

You may not be aware that the smile projects control, and that's exactly the kind of image that enhances your presence. Your smile makes people wonder, "What is he so happy about? Things must be going great for him." Naturally, we're more apt to be smiling when we don't have any troubles. When our lives are in order, we're much more likely to be wearing a smile. People will see your smile and think, "He must be doing something right."

Leaders must fill voids in others in order to lead. When people are fearful, leaders must provide reassurance and calm. When people are low in confidence, the leader must inspire. When people are lacking in motivation, the leader must provide the reason to act. The smile is a giving expression that leaders can use to fill a void in others.

Workplace environments can be very challenging. Employees are constantly carrying baggage from their personal lives into the office. While carrying this weight, they're expected to work with others and be cooperative with a can-do attitude. Their frame of mind is already more negative than it should be. Furthermore, the daunting challenges of achieving difficult work goals can compound their anxieties into a state of outright fear and worry.

What if one of your employees passes you in the hall when you have a sullen expression on your face? How will the employee feel? Most likely, the person will be negatively impacted by the image of you looking glum. "Why is the boss looking so down? Things must not be going well. The company must be in trouble.

Am I going to lose my job?" That's just one way that someone's imagination can spin out of control.

Another simple and more direct reaction might be, "Why is he always such a jerk to me? He never acknowledges me when I pass him in the hall. I'm not appreciated. He must not like me."

All the while, you may simply have a backache and aren't feeling chipper, or you're just feeling overly frustrated about a problem. Either way, your sullen-looking face had nothing to do with the employee you just failed to acknowledge. It wasn't anything personal, and the sky is not falling for the company. Guess what? No one can read your mind, so they fill in the blanks.

Smile Routinely

I've developed a consistent routine of maintaining a happy face around the office. If I have even the slightest look on my face that shows I'm not my usual upbeat self, someone will ask if everything is okay. The good thing about this situation is that my smile has established me as approachable. People feel comfortable with asking if I'm okay because they know I'm open. They don't have to read my mind, and therefore don't have to imagine why I'm not smiling. I can then tell them that there's no reason to worry, and I'm just deep in thought and all is well. The key is that I'm viewed as approachable because of my smile.

I once worked at a company where a senior manager I'll call Clint never smiled. I would pass him in the hallway maybe five times a day. I would say hello and he would barely look at me. One morning, I passed him in the hall and greeted him with a hearty, "Good morning, Clint!" He grunted. I felt lucky. He had at least acknowledged me.

I began to think of Clint as a crusty curmudgeon who was unapproachable and didn't care about his people. The best thing to do was avoid him. His lack of a personality severely limited his leadership ability. Clint's behavior set the tone for unpleasantness around the office. He was the kind of guy who was all about the numbers and didn't have time for pleasantries or anything else.

The most effective leaders are engaging. They take time to acknowledge others, and they are givers on an emotional level. They fill those emotional voids in their subordinates. The smile is the easiest way to give. It provides comfort, ease, reassurance, and more. These are all sensations that subordinates need to feel. Smiling is the best way to extend your presence.

---

4 Power Thoughts

1. Can you think of a superior who never smiles?
   a. How does it make you feel?
2. Are you willing to engage in two weeks of context-appropriate smiling around your workplace?
   a. Take notice of the effect it has on others.

CHAPTER 12

Your Most Valuable Currency

"The people when rightly and fully trusted will return that trust."

– Abraham Lincoln

T rust is your most valuable currency. There are two aspects to trust – honesty and reliability. Honesty is simple; people can take you at your word. Reliability means delivering on commitments. When you are given an assignment by your superiors or promise something to your subordinates, people can expect that it will be done on time and as promised.

Early in this book I said that honesty is the quality that subordinates expect most from a leader[5], according to extensive studies in the field of desired leadership qualities. Therefore, doing anything that damages trust is equivalent to playing with fire. When you strip away the prestige, titles, and position, all you have left is your professional reputation. You should never engage in any conduct that damages your reputation as an honest leader. It may be obvious but it's worth stressing – never lie to your superiors, subordinates, or customers. Once you've developed a reputation for deceit, your career – at least at your current employer and possibly elsewhere – is over. Re-establishing trust afterwards is almost impossible. I've witnessed and been on the receiving end of a broad range of "word parsing" in my career where people say

---

[5] Kouzes & Posner – The Leadership Challenge

they technically didn't lie, but the end result was deception anyway. This type of behavior is just as damaging to one's credibility. If you ever find yourself in a seemingly impossible situation, simply say you can't talk about that issue or you need time to collect your thoughts. That's always preferable to making promises you can't keep or fabricating a story.

Trust is Hard to Recover

Once a superior told me that senior management was committing to a specific business initiative I was heading. I was led to believe that I had a green light to proceed with my plans. Then the story began to drift. Suddenly, I was told that some members of my team would have to be "repurposed." Ultimately, more than half my team was reassigned, thereby crippling my plans. This resulted in a great deal of bitterness, and I could never trust that manager again. Sometimes managers are just weak leaders, and they fall back on deceit because they don't know how to deliver bad news to a subordinate. In the situation I just described, the superior was concerned that I might quit or encourage others to quit. In this case, the superior made a statement that sounded like commitment, but he didn't actually define the commitment. He deliberately allowed me to interpret the level of commitment for myself. Technically he didn't lie, but in fact he manipulated me with half-truths, rather than treating me as a partner and working to find a solution.

Trust is not only violated by direct lying, but also by negotiating in bad faith. You've probably experienced negotiating with colleagues. You think that you've finally reached an agreement, but then the stakeholders leave the bargaining table and do something other than what they said they would do. With your peers and colleagues, it's of utmost importance to follow through on your agreements. Don't leave the bargaining table intending to not fully implement your side of the agreement. Unfortunately this is a very routine occurrence, particularly where corporate politics is concerned. People often can't deal openly with each other for fear of confrontation. While initially uncomfortable, direct and open communication is the greatest trust-building exercise for coworkers in the long run.

Trust is a Two-Way Street

In the leader-subordinate relationship, you have to be trustworthy as a leader, but you also must be able to trust your subordinates. After all, you are staking your career on the results they attain. Dealing with dishonesty by subordinates is straightforward. If an employee blatantly and maliciously lies, he or she should be terminated. While this action may seem harsh, if you as leader are held to the highest of standards with regard to honesty, your subordinates should also adhere to the same high standards.

Sometimes dishonesty from subordinates is not malicious. They just have a hard time presenting facts objectively. Subordinates want desperately to be viewed favorably by their superiors and consequently may embellish facts in the hope of looking better. Unfortunately, this kind of exaggeration can be as detrimental to a leader and his organization as a blatant lie. Whether the hyperbole was intended maliciously or not, deceit is deceit and trust is the casualty.

You will frequently encounter the problem of word parsing when trying to pin down the facts. A great example of word parsing is: "It depends on what the meaning of the word 'is' is." Word parsing is not necessarily malicious, although it can be. Word parsing is an attempt by people to seek out meaning in communication that is suitable for their desired outcome. It's understandable for people to want clarity and comfort with the demands placed on them. In the context of leadership, you should expect your subordinates to parse "done" on a regular basis. When you ask, "What's the status of Project XYZ?" Don't be surprised if they quickly reply, "Oh, that's done." It would be wise to immediately ask, "What does done mean to you?"

You must clearly determine that the goals defined by your definition of "done" have actually been met. If your goals are not met, keep the subordinate engaged by requesting a review of current status. This engagement should take on a positive tone so that you don't perpetuate a culture where people become fearful of delivering bad news. Don't attack the messenger; instead, engage constructively and function as the catalyst for solutions.

Reliability

This brings us to the second aspect of trust – reliability. Your superiors want to know that when they hand an assignment to you, it will also, in fact, be done! Being reliable establishes organizational trust in you as someone who delivers. Clearly establish the goal when you're given an assignment and make sure whoever gives you the task spells out specifically what is expected of you. Describe your responsibilities for this task and send it back to the superior in an email for confirmation. Volunteer to provide regular updates on how things are going. Establish yourself as reliable. This approach enhances organizational respect for you and amplifies your presence by boosting your reputation for delivering results. You will then be trusted with more prestigious assignments by superiors, and your subordinates will reward you with their trust and loyalty because they know you are able to see your way through to accomplishing any endeavor.

Cultivate the same dependability in your subordinates. Set them up for success by clearly defining "done" and then working tirelessly to make sure they have the resources they need to complete the job. Weed out the chronic word parsers. They will fail, while wasting both time and money. If you see subordinates behaving like excuse factories, you have cause for concern. This behavior pattern is their M.O. for avoiding accountability.

Invest in Your People

You should demonstrate sincere concern for your subordinates' success. When they come to you with a problem, give them your undivided attention. Listening is the best way to build trust in a relationship. When people feel they have been heard, they feel validated and important. They will know you care, and they will put their trust in you. Gaining their trust is key to establishing your Power of Presence. Trust is what will help mitigate their fear when uncertainty and challenging times arise.

4 Power Thoughts

1. Do you trust your superiors? Why or why not?
2. Think about a time when you experienced deceit in the workplace. What were the consequences?
3. Are you viewed as trustworthy within your organization?
   a. What did you do to gain that trust?

CHAPTER 13

How to Inspire Your People

"A leader is a dealer in hope."

— *Napoleon Bonaparte*

How frequently have you heard the line, "hope is not a method"? This line became very popular within executive ranks after the publication of former Army Chief of Staff, General Gordon Sullivan's book with the same title. Through overuse, instead of focusing people on developing good methods, the phrase has mostly been adopted to ridicule expressions of hope. Indeed, hope is not a method, but we better keep hope in our method.

As a solitary ingredient, hope merely creates passive behavior as people stand around waiting for someone to show the way. On the other hand, an unenlightened manager is likely to say that people only want to hear a solid plan and ignoring any requirement to inspire his workforce is okay. However, just like hope alone is not enough to achieve a goal, neither is an unemotional process. People rise to the highest level of performance when you inject the appropriate range of emotion and enthusiasm along with a solid plan.

Inspiration Carries the Day

People really want to be inspired. People want to know they are making a difference. They also want to know what happens when things don't go well or the way forward becomes difficult. Hope and faith are the tools by which you inspire people to excel at the difficult tasks. It's what makes people keep marching toward a goal when their gut may be telling them that quitting could be a better option.

Leaders inspire people, while managers oversee things. Managers track inventory, supplies, and processes. They check things off their list and report the state of affairs. In contrast, leaders rally people. They inspire through hope and expressions of faith. It's disappointing that many managers completely ignore this component of their jobs. They are not comfortable with it. In fact, some don't think it's even part of their job.

Engaging in a new endeavor always carries with it some degree of anxiety. The loftier and more complicated the goal, the higher the anxiety will be. People are afraid of failure. Sadly, this fear is taught and reinforced throughout our formative years by our parents, schools, friends, and what we see in the media. The fear of failure becomes so intense that for many it becomes much easier to sit on the sidelines than to engage in a difficult pursuit.

When you want your team or organization to sign on to the pursuit of a challenging goal, be prepared to sell them on the attainability of the goal. Not only do you have to persuade on the basis of a sound technical plan as the roadmap, but you also have to sooth their deep-rooted fear of failure. This is the emotional component of leadership that managers tend to ignore. In their weakness, immature leaders simply resort to being taskmasters. Immature leaders are defined as leaders who have not yet fully mastered the techniques of effective leadership. Immature leaders can exist at any level in an organization.

Subordinates want to hear comments like, "I believe in you" or "I have confidence and faith in your ability to succeed." This is the rhetoric of hope and faith. Used properly, this communication will amplify your presence in your organization and work as an invisible guiding hand that nudges people forward, even when you're not there.

Hope is Powerful

Hope even saved a nation from invasion and conquest. When all seemed lost and the Nazis were on Great Britain's doorstep in 1940, Winston Churchill, the master speaker, inspired a nation with his hope-filled oratory. As John F. Kennedy would remark years later of Churchill's masterful speech craft:

"Churchill mobilized the English language and sent it into battle."

A more recent example of the potency of hope is how it was used to propel a virtually unknown junior senator into the White House. Barrack Obama's election was successful largely due to his relentless emphasis on a simple two-word slogan that evoked powerful images. With perfect tempo for nearly two years during his campaign, he relied on the impact of "Hope and Change." This simple theme tapped into people's dissatisfaction with a wide range of issues, their desire for change and their hopes for something better. Obama masterfully associated himself with the aspirations that hope conjures in people's minds.

Barrack Obama avoided defining hope. If he had defined hope, he would have diluted its impact as an emotionally charged word. Instead, he let each individual define hope for himself. This approach further enhanced the emotional response to his message by tapping the capacity of each person's imagination through the images in his speeches. A skillful speaker is able to fine-tune his message and deliver it effectively. By combining powerful images with highly effective speaking techniques, he can engage peoples' imagination into connecting their desires, their hopes, and their view of the future with him. Whether you agree with his politics or not, Barrack Obama's election is a case study in the masterful leveraging of hope as a tool for inspiration.

Tap the Power

Now envision what you can do when you tap the power of hope and faith in each of your subordinates. Imagine that you are an ethical leader who cares about the people you lead. Imagine that you have thought out a logical plan for success and then you stimulate your subordinates' sense of hope and faith that they will persevere through difficulty and overcome their obstacles. If you accomplish this, you will have an unstoppable workforce. To maximize your presence as a leader, always include expressions of hope and faith when rallying your team.

---

4 Power Thoughts

1. Have you ever been motivated by a supervisor who was inspirational?
   a. What did he or she do to inspire you? Can you model it?
   b. What was the work environment like?
2. Are people inspired in your current work environment?
   a. Why or why not?
3. Do you inspire people through hope when you lead?
   a. Recall the last time you inspired someone. How did you do it?
4. Use hope and faith to inspire someone you lead. Examine the outcome and reaction.

CHAPTER 14

How to Project Confidence

"Skill and confidence are an unconquered army."

– George Herbert
16th Century poet and orator

J ust like a good smile, confidence is magnetic. People are drawn to those who exude confidence. Showing confidence is essential to casting an effective presence as a leader. In contrast, subordinates respond adversely to timidity and reticence. The uneasy leader makes everyone uneasy. He is quickly judged as hypersensitive, indecisive, and possibly unstable. The leader who lacks confidence is comparable to a house with a shaky foundation. No one wants to enter that house.

Start an Epidemic

Confidence is contagious. It's up to you as a leader to start the epidemic! Not only must you display confidence, but in order to grow the effectiveness of your organization, you will need to boost the confidence of everyone around you.

Confidence must be genuine for a leader to be effective in spreading it throughout his team. It's hard to fake confidence for any period of time; the pretense will soon be uncovered. When you know who you are, what you can do, and you are grounded in your virtues and vision, confidence comes naturally. You can then project it outward through your calm demeanor, comforting smile, and sense of ease around others.

Project Confidence from Day One

The minute you are appointed to a position of leadership, your image as a confident leader will either be accepted or rejected. From the start, you must begin to assert your leadership. You must show that you're in charge, but there's a right and wrong way to do so. You don't want to be like the bull in a china shop or act like a new sheriff. In fact, the more bluster you rely on, the more likely others will perceive you as compensating for internal weakness. However, you do have to assert your authority without alienating your subordinates. Reticence in taking charge will make you appear lacking in self-confidence and undermine your presence.

During the early part of my career, I often hesitated in assuming the full role required by my position of authority. I can recall feeling unsure about how subordinates would respond to my direction. Later, I realized that I was uneasy because I incorrectly felt compelled to have all the answers. I would make some quick assessments, draw my own conclusions, and begin to take action.

As I matured as a leader, I looked back on those early days and laughed at how I ignored all the steps required to establish my presence as a confident leader. This uneasiness led me to want to quickly prove myself to people. Instead of asking questions and gaining a full picture of the situation, I would start to speak without first collecting facts. When you don't know what you're dealing with, how can you possibly feel at ease? Fortunately, over the years, I've developed a sure fire way to project confidence from the first moment I meet with subordinates.

Take Charge Naturally

If you've taken the time for the introspective journey required to gain poise, you will automatically project a calm sense of self. Subordinates will respond favorably to your calm inner leadership core with a sense of reassurance. They will be much more likely to accept you with an open mind. Your leadership presence will already have been boosted through this quality.

Begin your interactions by meeting individually with each team member who reports directly to you. Some of the more extroverted types will seek you out first. Embrace this. Start by asking questions about what they do. What problems do they see? Do they like their work? Then you may want to steer the conversation to their personal lives. Are they married and do they have a family? What are their hobbies? How do they like to spend their time when they are away from the office? Throughout the conversation, you should interact and share tidbits about your life to establish an open relationship. During these introductory sessions, take your time and don't rush through a conversation. The relaxed approach will add to the perception that you are in control of your time with minimal external pressure.

You may be wondering how these dialogues establish you as a confident leader. In fact, these conversations are very important. As the person asking the questions, you are in control of the conversation. The fact that you're steering the conversation subtly projects your authority. You are taking charge. If you find the subordinate grilling you with questions, reassume control of the conversation by injecting a question of your own or turning his inquiry around and ask what he thinks.

Also, showing your interest in the person's views establishes that you care. If you intently and actively listen, you are making your staff feel important. You are seen as approachable because you're having a conversation; you're not just barking orders at them. All these factors combined paint a picture of confidence.

After you've completed your rounds with at least the core members of your team, you will have learned a fair amount about any problems you may be facing. With these insights, you can then begin to formulate an action plan. You should request feedback from each team member regarding solutions to problems. How would they solve the problems? Be ready and willing to accept their ideas, if they make sense. Your openness to their thinking enhances your image as a confident person.

Some leaders mistakenly believe that if they accept an idea from a subordinate their leadership stature is somehow diminished. In reality, the opposite is true. Leadership stature is enhanced when you accept a subordinate's idea. You should look for opportunities to do so. Accepting other people's ideas is one of the best ways to instill confidence in your team.

Once you have feedback from your subordinates, present your high-level plan to the team. The existence of a plan and the beginnings of direction will go a long way toward the team placing their confidence in you. Your willingness to accept feedback demonstrates your inner confidence. It also shows that you are comfortable with dialogue and prefer persuasion to autocratic leadership.

Some years ago, I led a team that was responsible for managing a collection of government contracts. The team had been dispirited by a revolving door of managers, and the problem grew worse with the sudden departure of a recently appointed manager who took her "own people" with her.

I used this approach to win them over and establish my credibility. In a more subtle way, I was also showing authority. The feedback I received was, "You are the only manager that's ever come in here with a plan." They had placed their confidence in me because I displayed the self-assurance to first listen and understand their problems. I also took time to share the plan with them, giving them opportunity to comment. The approach I've described is a simple formula that serves as a great way to break the ice while taking the pressure off of you. With less pressure, you can be much more at ease in your leadership role.

Whenever you present your plans to your team, you should expect and even encourage dissent. When I hold a brainstorming session with a team of subordinates, I pointedly ask them, "Do you see any dumb ideas in this plan?" My bluntness demonstrates that I'm confident enough to ask the question. I've yet to have a subordinate reply with equal bluntness, "Yes, I see at least one dumb idea." However, the question nearly always opens dialogue to more suggestions. The dialogue also helps to reveal who is on board with the plan and who isn't.

Display Just the Right Amount of Gravitas

The most effective leaders have a tendency to appear as if they own the space they occupy. Much of this image is enhanced by their reputation and position. Leaders with gravitas generally give an impression that they are focused on important matters. You can observe this quality among business executives, politicians, and even athletes.

Just like Napoleon, George Washington could make his presence felt with a stare. His legend, stature, and manner enhanced his gravitas to a level beyond all his contemporaries. Physically, he was an imposing figure at 6 feet 2 inches and 230 pounds, but his stature as the hero of the American Revolution further amplified his gravitas. His contemporaries held him in the highest regard because of his sacrifice and loyalty to the nation. He had led his army to victory often by the sheer force of his personality. He played to this legend by maintaining a cool distance in public and by using symbols of power in just the right measure. For example, when traveling across country in the post-war period, he would ride in a carriage. Just before entering a town, he would leave the carriage and mount his white stallion for a regal entry that projected his gravitas. Washington understood gravitas and used it to his advantage to project his leadership presence.

In projecting confidence, develop your gravitas as a means of furthering your leadership presence. Don't overdo it or you will come off looking ridiculous. Save your humor for the well-timed witty remark that actually enhances your gravitas by displaying your mental acuity without sacrificing dignity. Avoid slapstick style silliness or any behavior that is a net negative to your gravitas. Display gravitas in a manner that is contextually appropriate. For example, if you have just been promoted to the leadership position for a team of accounts receivable clerks, you don't want to project an image that says you're the chief financial officer. However, you should distance yourself from the crowd and begin projecting an image that you deal with important issues. This behavior style will help to project your image as a leader and as someone who is ready for a higher position. Be subtle but clear in separating yourself from the rank and file without demeaning anyone.

You're Not That Important

Displaying a sense of humor as well as the ability to laugh at oneself shows your inner security and confidence. If you make a mistake that draws laughter, the best thing to do is laugh along. Becoming embarrassed or angry merely reveals your insecurity. Don't take yourself so seriously that you can't laugh at your own goof-ups. You're not that important.

When I was a lieutenant in the Army, I was assigned an extra duty of leading a company of about 150 soldiers in a monthly parade. Our company had never won the review competition and I wanted to change that. I contacted the first sergeant and arranged practice drills. When we had finished our rehearsal, I asked him to do it again so we could nail down our turns and timing to perfection. At the conclusion of practice, we looked and felt great.

The parade day finally arrived, and there I was out front giving the orders and feeling confident. We executed flawlessly. We passed the reviewing stand and snapped perfect salutes; we were in step and looking sharp. Once past the reviewing stand, I needed to move the company to a holding area so the soldiers could be dismissed. I spotted a location up ahead and immediately called for a column right. I personally executed a perfect and immediate column left! Everyone went right and there I was heading left all by myself. It was a classic comedy moment. One of the other officers acted quickly, took control of the company, and brought everyone to a halt. Once I made my way back to the front of the company, I ordered everyone to stand at ease. Immediately, the entire company burst out in laughter. I started laughing right along with them and told them to enjoy the moment because it was indeed outrageously funny.

My display of confidence by demonstrating that I could laugh at myself was the best possible way to deflect true ridicule while providing a great moment for morale boosting. Leverage these moments by demonstrating your confidence and laughing at yourself. The more you display your confidence, the more your presence will grow and your leadership will be respected.

Know Your Stuff

Confidence is also derived from a strong sense of competence and experience. To lead effectively, you must have absolute commitment to learning and enhancing your level of knowledge regarding key functions that make you effective in your job. For example, if you're a supervisor in a manufacturing facility, you should learn as much as you can about the end-to-end processes in sufficient detail. You should be the one who is thinking about contingencies if things go wrong. As the leader, you must be the one who gives direction in a crisis. You can only do this confidently if you know what you're doing. However, you should not feel like you have to know all the answers. But as the leader, you must know enough about your work to gauge the impact of your decisions and direction at all times. The only way to do that is to maintain a suitable level of knowledge and competence in your field and job function.

4 Power Thoughts

1. How did you feel during times when you worked for a manager that lacked confidence?

   a. Was the work environment productive?

2. In situations where the leader lacks confidence, what do you think the consequences will be?

3. What personal changes can you make to become a confident leader?

CHAPTER 15

Empower More – Control Less

"[A leader] must walk a tightrope between the consent he must win and the control he must exert."

– Vince Lombardi

E ffective leadership presence requires the proper balance between control and trust. A poised leader does not try to control everything, because he knows that excessive control is a manifestation of insecurity, not poise. A poised leader has the inner confidence to establish his presence by empowering others, sharing control, and conveying trust to his subordinates.

You don't have to control everything to be a successful leader. You want to guide without maintaining direct control. Focus on establishing and continuously shaping the underlying operating culture instead. Shaping your team's culture requires the imprint of your well-grounded leadership personality. Your organization will be a reflection of who you are. As you've seen already, the core of the culture you establish must be based on a solid adherence to virtues. Focus on virtue and build the right values that lead to sound principles. With this approach, the number of required rules can be minimized to only what is absolutely necessary.

Unskilled leaders make the common mistake of trying to have a rule for everything in an effort to control as much as possible. The reality is that you can't control everything no matter how hard you try, and the more you try to control, the more you'll find yourself in the role of enforcer instead of leader.

The more rules you have, the more you have to enforce. Failure to enforce a rule makes a leader look weak, undisciplined, and potentially unjust if the rule is not enforced uniformly. The more rules you have, the more vulnerable you are to inconsistency. The rules constrain you as much as they constrain the people you're trying to control. Having too many rules actually weakens your leadership presence.

Know Your ROLE

Years ago, I developed an approach while coaching youth sports that I still apply today in corporate life. On the first day of practice, I would hand out a sheet of paper to each player that said, "Know your ROLE!" I would stress that the team only had four rules to remember – Respect, On-time, Listening, and Effort. Living one's ROLE was required of the coach (leader) as well as all teammates. If these rules were broken, I would explain the consequences in terms of how the team would be hurt. I avoided assigning a silly penalty to each infraction that I would then be required to enforce. I had very few headaches with my approach compared to the other coaches, who often became screaming hotheads when their players didn't follow their rules. ROLE represents a set of guidelines on which you can build your culture. Let's examine the applicability of ROLE in corporate life.

Respect in the workplace is essential. Without it, you won't have any functioning business relationships. You can't demand respect; you're not automatically entitled to it. You earn respect by giving respect and being respectable. Once you grant respect to those around you, it will be lavished upon you in return. If you're not treated with respect, you have the moral high ground to demand an explanation for the disrespectful behavior.

Being on time means always striving for punctuality – for meetings, deadlines, and achieving goals. Lateness means disrespect for your colleagues and subordinates, and ultimately, loss of respect for you. Being on time is a core requirement of business effectiveness. As with many organizational characteristics, the leader establishes the behavioral norm. Unfortunately, lack of punctuality is glaringly common among leaders.

Listening means you use your ears far more than your mouth and you take extra care to understand others. Listening improves communication quality and solves more problems than you can imagine.

Effort requires that you, as a team member, give 100% to everything you do. If something is worth doing, it is worth doing right. Effort is the force that achieves all desired results. The ROLE approach keeps things simple, while also setting the right expectations.

You may be wondering how to move from team culture building to actually getting things done. You need a few more pieces to the leadership puzzle. After all, no organization can function effectively without verification and accountability.

Implement Rational Controls

In the corporate world, a reasonable level of control is required to ensure that important actions are indeed completed with the desired result. There are also many required controls that are mandated by law. Here I'm focusing on discretionary controls that a leader must implement that relate to production of the product or service a company sells. In this context, control is most effectively exercised through process and persuasion. People need to understand what they are supposed to do. The *what* should come from you – the leader who sets the goals. However, you should strive to have your subordinates develop the *how* as much as possible. Being invested in developing how things are accomplished produces a rewarding sense of empowerment and ownership for your workforce. It will also help you identify the thinkers and those who have initiative in your organization. Those who can't figure out the "how" are usually not proactive people and function better as task executors rather than task leaders.

The implementation of rational controls in your organization can be simplified to four steps - Plan, Teach, Agree, and Check (PTAC). Your plan must set clear goals. Let your team have input into how the goals are achieved. As you design your plan, remember that all processes you develop to achieve your overall goal must include feedback loops. Feedback is essential for you to check on the effectiveness of whatever work is being performed. You should design checkpoints in your work plans to create opportunities to provide feedback. Chapter 26 covers planning in greater detail.

An effective leader teaches the work processes to all involved. This ensures that everyone understands his or her functions and responsibilities. Teaching work processes also establishes the boundary lines. Let people know where the boundary lines are and that they must check in with you when the boundary lines are about to be breached. As long as their decisions result in staying inside the boundary lines that you've established, you're far better off empowering your subordinates to make those decisions.

Next, gain agreement. If everyone buys in to the approach, the control you must exercise becomes less taxing. Since everyone is working to a plan voluntarily, you won't have to play enforcer as much. This frees up valuable time that can be spent coaching your subordinates on how to achieve excellent results. You should agree on the set of metrics with your team in advance to ensure that expectations are properly established.

Last, check on progress with your team. Review the established metrics to ensure the expected results are being attained. Depending on the results and feedback sessions, you can course-correct any plan as needed. Use feedback sessions as an opportunity to make your team more confident and drive them forward. This expression of confidence has the added benefit of asserting your presence.

Bureaucracy Smothers Initiative

During my career, I have worked in organizations where there was a rule for everything and nearly everything had to be approved by upper management. In the worst cases, the rules required as many as seven signatures to gain approval to proceed. Organizations mired in such bureaucracy become slow, lumbering institutions in a world where nimble organizations are increasingly winning market share. Workforce morale is usually low because people feel constrained and unable to exercise any creative control over their work.

Recently, a colleague told me a story about his manager. When my colleague was delivering some suggestions and insights recommending how their work should be done, the manager responded, "You know, I had a boss once who took all my ideas and threw them in the trash right in front of me. He then proceeded to explain to me that my job was to do what he told me. Now I'm telling you. Just do what I tell you and don't worry about anything else." Can you imagine how stifling this sort of leadership is? Establish solid core principles first. The necessary detailed rules for performance will flow naturally from there. Empower your people to the greatest extent possible. Use checkpoints to stay on course. Your minimalist approach to rules and control will reinforce your presence as a confident leader. Your people will feel empowered, trusted, and appreciated.

---

4 Power Thoughts

1. Have you ever worked for a control freak?

   a. How long did it take you to quit?

2. Describe a work environment you were part of where there were very few rules.

   a. How did you feel about working there?

3. When authority is taken away from you or curtailed, how does that make you feel?

4. On the other hand, when your authority is increased, how do you feel?

CHAPTER 16

How to Become the Next Great Communicator

"Congress can make a general, but only communication makes him a commander."

– U.S. Army Signal Corps wisdom

Without effective communication, leaders just can't lead. Developing as a leader requires that you invest time and effort into improving your ability to communicate comfortably in a variety of settings. These settings include one-on-one, group meetings, and the large audience. Today, leaders at the highest levels must also master communication over multimedia technology. The management of geographically dispersed workforces and the fast-paced competitive environment make multimedia communication tools indispensable to a leader. I highly recommend that you pursue training on how to uses these tools effectively. In this chapter, you will learn about communication skills required in the three in-person settings.

Your words must provide positive reinforcement of your leadership presence. When you speak as the leader, your words should carry weight. Like an overabundance in supply of anything, the more you speak, the cheaper your words become. Therefore, your words should always be chosen carefully for the right impact at all times. You should sound confident and authoritative without

129

sounding dictatorial. If you project a confident image with strong gravitas, and don't back it up when you speak, people will detect an incongruity between your image and what you say. The result will be a rapidly diminishing leadership presence. Let's now examine some scenarios for leadership dialogue that are often challenging for leaders of all experience levels.

One-on-One Settings

The one-on-one setting creates a special communication dynamic. Some leaders are uncomfortable in one-on-one situations because it feels too personal. Asserting presence in a group discussion can be easier because attention is naturally divided among various parties and the air of formality places focus on the leader's formal authority.

Have you ever met with a senior leader in a group and then the room emptied as the meeting ended? Maybe then you were unexpectedly left alone with that leader. Did you experience the sudden "shift in the air"? You probably felt tenser being alone with the senior leader. Guess what? He or she probably did too. Some leaders are not as comfortable handling the communication flow, which now must be carried by just two parties.

On the other hand, a leader who is totally self-assured and enjoys personal interaction with others can easily shift to a more personal dialogue when meeting individually with subordinates. Relaxing and projecting a feeling that you are comfortable in your own skin sets the tone for positive interaction. Chances are that your subordinate will be a bit more on edge than you. Your ability to relax and welcome the interaction will place anyone who meets with you at ease.

Listening Builds Trust – In any setting that requires personal interaction, demonstrating that you are actively listening to your subordinate cultivates trust. Be sure to listen with empathy and focus on key words your subordinate uses to express his or her thoughts. Minimize the amount of thinking you do while your subordinate is speaking. If you spend most of your time formulating your thoughts for a response while your subordinate is speaking, you will not fully absorb the gist of what they are trying to say. Your concern may be, "If I don't set the wheels in my mind turning while the other person is speaking, how can I respond?"

Most people fear "dead air" in conversation. Therefore, you tend to want to quickly respond to avoid the possibility of awkward silence. In reality, you should use a bit of silence as an advantage. The approach is easier than you think. People routinely underestimate the speed of their mind. You can take advantage of silence gaps that you inject into your verbal communication.

When your subordinate stops speaking, you should use the power of the pause. Stop and ponder the key words you heard. Your pause will enhance trust with your subordinate because it demonstrates that you are giving careful consideration to what he or she has said. The pause is the first *time gap technique*. You will be amazed at how fast your mind will process what you heard when you are calm and quiet for just a few moments. If you're at a loss for words, you can use the second time gap technique – rephrase what you heard and ask a question. By rephrasing, I mean that you take the key words you heard and repeat them back in the form of a question to gain confirmation that you understood what was being said. The question gives you more time to think. Following this simple communication protocol will strengthen the meaningfulness of your one-on-one interactions and enhance your presence as an empathetic leader.

The Basic Opener – When I meet one-on-one, I immediately make the conversation personal without sacrificing professional distance. I usually start with asking, "How are you?" Then, I directly follow up with, "How are things going for you?" Or, "What are you focusing on lately?" I then pause and deliberately wait for an answer. This shows that I'm genuinely interested and not just making small talk. We then move on to specifics of the business at hand. You should be aware that sometimes you'll ask, "How are you?" and your subordinate will launch into a detailed account of a difficult personal life situation. Remember, you opened that conversation thread, so you should patiently listen or you risk coming off as insensitive. Now, let's take a look at some typical one-on-one leadership situations.

The Venting Subordinate – There will come a time when a subordinate will burst into your office and verbally unload. He or she may be angry with you, upset about a situation involving co-workers, or frustrated over a project. It will take practice, but you should do your best to stay absolutely calm. Nothing that some-one says in a business setting can physically hurt you. Maintain your composure no matter what. When it becomes evident that an employee needs to vent, your best response is, "Go ahead, I'm listening."

Patiently listening to problems or criticism from subordinates will build trust and, again, boost your confident image. At times, they may be angry and upset, but unless they cross the line of common decency and respect, let them talk. Don't feel threatened. Ask questions and listen actively. Don't be drawn into a debate that spirals downward and diminishes your presence. Remain in control of your emotions. Respond when you're ready. If you are particularly upset by what the other person has said, politely but firmly disengage from the conversation. You can thank the indi-viduals for their input and let them know that you want to care-fully consider what they've said and that you'll resume the conversation at some future point.

Often, if subordinates think they were out of line with their outburst, they will come in and apologize before you have a chance to get back in touch with them. In these cases, tell them it's water under the bridge as long as their behavior is not a routine occurrence. Everyone has a hard day. Then provide the feedback you promised. Level with them. Even if it's not what they want to hear, honesty will be appreciated in the long run.

At any point, you can take control of a conversation and direct it toward a productive and meaningful exchange. You can gain control by asking simple questions. For example, "So I understand that you're having problems with the shipping department. Have you spoken to anyone about the issue? What did they say?" You can easily put the brakes on the conversation and steer it the way you need it to go by asking questions.

There is an almost infinite array of scenarios for leadership dialogue in one-on-one settings, but there are two scenarios that are specifically troublesome to many leaders. These are: discussing performance issues and firing someone. These two situations are examples of what I call the "difficult conversations."

If you know you're going to have a difficult conversation, meet it head on. Don't dance around the issue. Doing so will only lead to loss of respect and diminished presence. I'll address the performance issue first. Here's one example on how I deliver the assessment of poor performance:

Discussing Poor Performance – I usually skip the personal pleasantries during these sessions. "Bill, thanks for stopping in. I'm going to cut right to the chase. I want you to know that you do many things well around here, and I believe you have the capacity to be successful. However, I've noticed that you've been consistently late on your deadlines. I welcome the opportunity to discuss this problem with you. I hope you understand that this lateness issue is hurting everyone on the team, and it can't continue. I believe I've been very clear with all our team members on the importance of meeting our deadlines. I would really like to know what has been causing the problem and what we can do to ensure your performance meets our standards."

What generally happens next is either the employee acknowledges the problem and apologizes or offers a litany of excuses. Either response can be a deflection mechanism by the subordinate. If a litany of excuses ensues, the individual is likely not accepting responsibility. However, it is possible that he or she may produce valid reasons of which you were not aware that somehow explain the problem. You need to do your homework in advance so that you have all the facts straight prior to engaging in performance-related discussions. The "excuse factory" employee will likely be back to his or her old failure pattern in short order following your conversation. However, in most cases, subordinates care deeply about their performance, and many do correct their behavior and improve the quality of their work. They usually appreciate that you told them their performance was below standards.

I generally conclude the performance counseling session with a statement similar to this: "Bill, I know this hasn't been an easy conversation, but it's my responsibility to be honest with you about your performance. I hope you can appreciate that, and I know you don't want to have this sort of conversation again."

You can certainly use your own choice of words, but the structure of the statement above is very important. The phrase, "It's my responsibility to be honest," is extremely powerful in this setting. It elevates your presence as an authentic leader who means business. Remember that honesty is a priority for subordinates. You are therefore playing your strongest card when you align yourself with honest communication.

The next most important part of the statement is, "I know you don't want to have this sort of conversation again." This phrase is essential because it carries a double meaning. It can mean that no one wants to have another unpleasant conversation, but it also implies that next time there will be consequences if the poor performance is repeated. You should accompany this part of the statement with direct eye contact; don't speak until you receive a response. The statement sets the subordinate's "wheels" spinning and has a lasting impact that reinforces that you are serious.

Under no circumstances should you include an "or else" type of threat. A stated or implied threat turns the conversation unnecessarily negative. It's counterproductive to what you are trying to achieve, which is corrective action. An "or else" threat also locks you into a promised action that you may regret and want to reconsider later on, but if you do reconsider, then you will be viewed as inconsistent and weak. Avoid the "or else." It's best left to the imagination. Now let's address the other tough conversation – dismissing a subordinate.

Dismissing an Employee – In corporate life, leaders dread dismissing employees more than anything. On an emotional level, they subconsciously tend to equate firing with death. Because of this, I've seen far too many managers either delegate the responsibility of firing someone to a subordinate, or they procrastinate to an extent that makes the situation much worse for everyone involved. In their effort to dodge the discomfort of firing someone, weak leaders often pass a problem employee off to another department. I've seen low performers extend their careers for years before the system finally caught up with them. This is very detrimental to an organization. Don't fail as a leader by avoiding tough conversations.

In contrast, I equate firing with rebirth, not death. When you have reached a point where you feel the need to fire an employee, most likely, no one is happy. You're unhappy with the employee's performance, and the employee is probably not drawing any satisfaction or sense of worth from his job. Therefore, why not create rebirth by opening up new possibilities for both you and the subordinate? This is the key to this difficult conversation. Of course, you must make sure that you have spoken with your colleagues in Human Resources and Legal departments in advance. Then you can proceed with the conversation as follows:

"Bill, thanks for stopping in. I want you to know that you are a decent guy. However, if we want to be totally honest with each other, you can't possibly be happy here. I'm not happy and you're not happy. Your performance has been sorely lacking, and it has not improved despite our numerous conversations. It's best for both of us if we part ways. Regrettably, the company will be letting you go effective [insert date]."

"I understand that this may come as a blow to you, but I believe it is the start of much better things in your life and not just the end of a job. I see some really strong qualities in you that I think you can leverage in future employment. You are [insert lots of compliments]. I'm confident you will land on your feet."

Maybe I've been lucky, but I've never had this conversation blow up on me. In fact, every time I've delivered this dismissal, the subordinate has actually thanked me. Why? The positive reaction came because I was completely honest, and *I let the employees exit with their dignity intact.* This is significant. Don't ever rob people of their dignity in this situation; if you do, it could get ugly.

You may have a negative reaction to the approach described above and potentially view it as manipulative. Nothing could be further from the truth as long as you're honest about what you're saying. Additionally, your role as a leader is to give. You must always be the source of hope, optimism, and vision. This approach delivers all three qualities at a time when one of your subordinates needs it most. Tough conversations are part of leader's job. Be compassionate. Your presence will be enhanced if you learn to handle the tough conversations well. This next one-on-one scenario is easier because it's pleasant, but surprisingly many leaders still fail to handle it effectively.

Delivering Positive Feedback – Telling a subordinate that he or she is doing a great job or that you appreciate all the hard work the person has done is one of the most pleasant and rewarding parts of being a leader. Yet many leaders don't devote enough time to communicating positive feedback to their teams. Remember the quote, "A leader is a dealer in hope." Delivering positive feedback is an opportunity to inspire. Take the time to inspire people. It is a core function of leadership. When delivering positive feedback, make your statements heartfelt and be specific about what is going right. Tell people you've definitely noticed their great work and that it is highly appreciated. It is amazing how much this lifts people up.

I once worked for a senior executive who was generally an effective leader. However, he was a bit of an introvert, and the demands of his job kept him glued to his desk and focused on managing upward in the organization. On a rare occasion, he actually came to one of our project war rooms and told everyone how much he appreciated the long hours and focused effort. The result was amazing. One of the project team members who reported to me was elated.

Giving positive feedback is powerful. However, like anything, too much of a good thing is counterproductive. Therefore, don't give positive feedback excessively, gratuitously, or disingenuously. Otherwise, you will dilute its positive effect and actually diminish your presence by seeming to patronize your people. Give positive feedback from the heart and deliver it when it's appropriate.

Group Settings

Meetings with team members and stakeholders ranging from three to thirty people are very common group settings in which leaders communicate. These meetings are held to exchange information or make decisions. Regardless of the context, the first and most important rule is to start the meeting on time!

Be respectful of others by recognizing their time as valuable. Make sure that technology, such as a conference bridge or laptop with projector, is set up in advance. This will ensure everything starts on time and others don't have to watch you scurry about as you plug in your equipment or arrange the chairs.

Leaders who habitually show up late to meetings they've organized are telling their subordinates that their time isn't valuable. You would be amazed how often this happens at all levels of corporations. Not only is it disrespectful, but also the multiplied financial impact in lost productivity is enormous.

Everyone is late on occasion, but the habitually tardy leader risks being viewed as arrogant or someone whose life is out of control. In either case, the negative impression on subordinates diminishes your presence. Subordinates must view their leaders as being able to manage time effectively. Starting your meetings on time sets the proper pace for your organization. Punctuality is the first enabler for productive communication, and your people will appreciate you for it.

If you want to have meaningful communication, all devices must be put away. While these devices have boosted productivity and are very convenient, they also inhibit your ability to focus on the task at hand. Think about the message you are sending to your subordinates when they're speaking to you, but you're checking your messages or responding to someone who just texted you.

Is this living your ROLE? Is it respect for one another? Is your leadership presence enhanced by this behavior? No, no, and no.

Commit to leaving your cell phone on your desk during a meeting, or at least in your pocket on silent mode. Adopting this behavior will enhance your presence by communicating that what is being said in the meeting is important to you.

The Brainstorming Session – In a brainstorming session, a group of people gathers to discuss issues, plan a course of action, and make a decision. If you're the host of a brainstorming session, set the agenda and objectives in advance. Clearly define the desired outcome of the meeting. Define any "out of bounds" conditions, such as topics to avoid at this particular stage or unnecessary detail that is to be addressed in a later discussion.

Once these preliminaries have been completed, be the catalyst for the discussion by asking probing, open-ended questions to get the conversation moving. Then step back. As the leader, you may have an idea of where you want your team to go with regard to a specific solution or issue, but you should avoid injecting your views too early and nixing your team's ideas. If you consistently veto everyone's input, people will just yield to your authority and close down. Instead, help to guide your team toward the answer you think achieves the organizational goal. Ensuring that your team members contribute to the solution will make them feel as if the solution was their idea. They will surprise you with how much they will build on a solution, even in cases where you already knew the direction you wanted to take. In many cases, they will give you a brilliant idea that you hadn't considered.

What do you do when the way forward is not immediately clear to you? You need time to think and digest facts. You also don't want to appear indecisive and lost. Let your team help you without damaging your presence. During your brainstorming sessions, gain wisdom through silence.

There's an excellent example from history where silence was practiced with maximum effect. Let's examine the Constitutional Convention - the ultimate brainstorming session that established America's enduring constitution. During the convention, Benjamin Franklin distinguished himself as the de facto leader, though he would remain silent for extended periods. Sometimes, the other members thought he had fallen asleep. Then, at just the right moment, he would rise to his feet and either ask a series of very pointed questions or make a profound comment that would captivate the attention of other members.

Franklin was an ardent believer in the Socratic Method, which is simply the application of logic through questioning until a suitable answer is received. His questions allowed him to subtly lead and gently guide the discussion without appearing as though he were trying to force his own ideas through the committee. His periods of silence gave him time to ponder alternatives while digesting the facts and opinions he heard. Through this approach of directed questioning and timely comments, Franklin established himself as the group's sage. No one would consider moving to the next issue until he had weighed in.

The "wisdom through silence" approach may seem counterintuitive. How can keeping quiet actually make you look smart? It works because you are letting the time gap techniques work for you. First, the approach takes the spotlight off of you by diffusing the need for you to have all the answers. The time to think allows you to calmly formulate your thought processes without being absorbed in defending your every statement. Secondly, the approach allows you to engage in active listening so you can digest what others are saying. As the team engages in point and counterpoint, you can stoke the conversation with timely questions while you buy time to weigh the pros and cons of alternatives. When your team has exhausted its debate or reached an impasse, you can then express a few observations, preferences, or reservations about a specific approach.

When the time for a decision arrives, usually one option will stand out above others. You can then select it as the preferred course of action and ask for any last minute dissenters to speak up. If there is dissent, hear the person out without being condescending or dismissive.

Subordinates and peers will sometimes try to argue with you for several reasons. They may simply be exhibiting genuine dissent with the best interests of the team at heart. Alternatively, they may have less benevolent reasons. They may be testing your character, engaging in pedantry, or they could be the resident naysayer burdened with a persistently negative outlook. The ultimate way to defuse persistent dissent is to ask the dissenter to propose a solution. No one has the right to just torpedo ideas and walk away. If someone torpedoes an idea, he or she should contribute an answer. This approach projects your leadership while drawing ideas out of people and avoiding confrontation.

Regardless of the type of dissent you encounter, don't let people filibuster your meetings. Avoid a degrading argument that diminishes respect for your role or drags you down to the level of your opponent. Few situations can degrade the presence of a leader more than arguing publicly with a subordinate or peer. Never appear to take anything personally. This will only show everyone that you are thin skinned and insecure. If you believe that there has been a transgression that is rooted in a lack of respect for you, deal with it privately.

Here's an example. In the consulting business, we fill out timesheets to account for all our billable time. Once, I was recommending a time charging procedure to my team and a subordinate called my recommendation unethical in front of all my direct reports. Because I knew and respected the individual, I did not take his blunt statement personally, although I could have taken it as an affront. He just didn't choose his words carefully. I could easily have lashed back and interpreted his comment as directly impugning my honesty. Instead, I maintained my cool and assured him and the team that the procedure was indeed ethical, but to make everyone feel comfortable, I said I would consult the head of Human Resources. As it turned out, I was correct. I followed up with the specifics of the procedure and gently corrected the individual in private. This approach enhanced my leadership presence because I handled the challenge without arguing and maintained my composure.

The general flow of leadership communication for group settings I have described above is not meant to be a rigid cookbook approach. These are merely tips based on proven techniques that have worked well. Just remember, it's your job to man the helm, not to have all the answers. Guide your team members to reach the intended conclusions so that you merely approve them. They will feel empowered, validated, and valued. In turn, you avoid catching all the arrows while enhancing your presence at the same time. *The best way to maximize the impact of your words is to listen carefully to your subordinates and then speak last.*

The Information Exchange – If someone is briefing you, most of the dynamics will be similar to the brainstorming session, except that there is no immediate pressure to drive the agenda toward a decision. Therefore, the information exchange is typically less tense than the brainstorming meeting. You will want to do some homework in advance to understand the briefing subject so you'll be able to ask intelligent questions. The listening skills and questioning approach is essentially also the same as the brainstorming session.

If you are the presenter in the information exchange, then you need to prepare a few extra steps. Make sure you know the hot-button issues that may arise. Do the background checking with key members in the group so you know in advance how they will react to your information. The last thing you want is to be blindsided by an adverse reaction to what you are presenting.

Next, leave time for Q&A and solicitation of feedback from the group. Recognize that you may receive questions from the group for which you do not have an answer or are not able to give an answer because of time or other restrictions. To maintain your presence, don't start fumbling to make up an answer on the spot or give an answer to something you can't discuss. Telling attendees that you do not have an answer at present is far less damaging to your presence than fumbling. The point is that you are a leader, and leaders are in control of their communication at all times. Say that you will get an answer back to the team as soon as possible. If you can't discuss the topic, just say so. People will respect this approach much more than fumbling.

The Audience Setting

I define the audience setting as the typical public speaking environment. This is the environment where you can truly shine as a leader. Speaking to an audience is the setting that is most powerful for enhancing your presence and provides maximum opportunity for shaping culture, communicating vision, and delivering inspiration. Words are the basic components for communication, but a leader elevates presence most powerfully through visual and emotional methods. In public speaking, you learn to align your words with what people see and feel about you as a leader. The most impactful speakers combine vivid imagery with appropriate body language to ensure the audience feels the emotion they wish to convey. As you rise in the ranks of leadership, the importance of this skill set will increase significantly. Public speaking gives you a significant confidence boost and thereby enhances your presence by leaps and bounds. It also gives you visibility in your professional circles thereby creating career opportunities.

Delving into all the techniques associated with effective public speaking is beyond the scope of this book. Two excellent sources of additional information and training in public speaking are Toastmasters and the National Speakers Association (NSA). Toastmasters is an instructional, non-profit organization that is a forum for practicing your public speaking skills. The NSA is an association for professional speakers and can be a great source for locating experienced speech coaches. Public speaking is not something you can master overnight. Therefore, start working on your skills as soon as possible to ensure you will be ready when a speaking opportunity arises.

Always do your homework about your audience. Know the issues and know how they feel about them. Conveying passion and genuine emotion about your message is fundamental to effectiveness in public speaking. As for speech crafting, my favorite book on the subject is *Speak Like Churchill, Stand Like Lincoln* by James C. Humes.

Speak Well - Lead Well

Mastering appropriate leadership communication is essential to extending your leadership presence. Your words should be well-chosen and well-timed through active listening followed by the wise question or comment at the right moment. Through practice, develop comfort in both group and one-on-one settings. Use questions to control the flow of a conversation. Don't shy away from difficult conversations. Meeting tough situations head on enhances your presence; avoiding them only projects weakness. Your mastery of leadership communication will allow you to speak with authority while fully integrating your image as a strong, self-assured leader. Master the medium of public speaking for maximum enhancement of your leadership presence. Effective communication is a core leadership skill. If you can't communicate, you can't lead.

---

4 Power Thoughts

1. Think of situations where you observed ineffective leadership communication.
   a. What was the scenario?
   b. What impression did it give you of the leader?
2. Have you experienced a situation where your leadership dialogue was ineffective?
   a. What could have done better?
3. Do you know any supervisors or leaders who consistently project a strong leadership presence through their dialogue?
   a. What impressions do they make on you?
   b. What specific techniques do they use that makes them effective?
4. Join Toastmasters, NSA, or hire a speaking coach. Amplify your leadership presence and maximize your effectiveness as a leader by polishing your public speaking skills.

CHAPTER 17

Relationships with Superiors and Subordinates

"Show me a man who is a good loser, and I'll show you a man who is playing golf with his boss."

– Jim Murray

A leader will thrive or fail depending on the health of organizational relationships above and below him. You must maintain and nurture these relationships to enhance your leadership presence. Here are the tips you need to succeed.

Your Relationship With Your Superior

It doesn't matter who you are – everyone in the management chain of a 21st century corporation has to answer to someone. Even if you're the CEO, you have to answer to your board. Learning the skills needed to maintain positive relationships with the people you answer to is critical to your success.

Act like you belong – Generally, you'll gain more respect from your superior if you act as if you are capable of interacting with him at his social level. This doesn't mean you treat him as if he was a peer or a team member. It also does not mean that you refuse to commit to his or her authority. Instead, you need to project your presence in such a way that says you are a capable leader who understands the issues that your superior regularly confronts. You are striving to create mutual ease and comfort in your business interactions with your superior. Be knowledgeable about the terminology your superior uses and subject matter he discusses within your business setting. Demonstrate your capability and willingness to accept responsibility to resolve his most pressing concerns.

By projecting a steady but not overpowering stature, you can make your superior feel more at ease. He will begin to feel like he is interacting with someone who is on the same level in terms of mutual interests and capabilities. This is a tried and true behavior-mirroring technique for rapport building. If you act too humbly or subservient, your superior won't think of you as someone worthy of greater responsibility. When opportunities arise, you will be overlooked because you have presented a weak image. In contrast, working as if you belong at the same level establishes and maintains mutual respect. Your superior will consider you as someone who can be relied upon to accept greater responsibility.

Play it safe at first – Before you get to know your superior, assume that your boss may be an underdeveloped leader or may have a very sensitive ego. Sometimes you'll be "lucky" enough to have a boss who is both underdeveloped and sensitive. Lack of development and a delicate ego are traits that often go hand-in-hand. As you get to know your superiors better, you'll be able to assess their level of leadership development. Do they exhibit the levels of poise and presence you expect to find in leaders? With a few conversations, you'll be able to form an initial assessment. The degree of sensitivity will dictate how carefully you must handle your communications with your superior.

There's a significant correlation between seniority in the leadership chain and ego sensitivity. The higher a leader is in the management chain, the more sensitive he or she is to circumstances that impact ego. The reason for this correlation is that the more senior a leader is, the more removed he is from the majority of his constituents and subordinates. Therefore, image becomes more important because few people have direct contact with the leader. Anything that makes the leader "look bad" is usually met with severe repercussions. These circumstances can give rise to a highly sensitive ego. Only a skilled and self-assured leader can maintain a well-regulated ego while managing the necessities of maintaining the proper image for his organization.

Make the boss look good – Don't outshine your superior by boasting about an accomplishment before the person has had an opportunity to inform his or her superiors. Instead, give your superior the opportunity to collect credit from those above him and to acknowledge you in due course. A superior who is an effective leader will publicly shower subordinates with credit at the appropriate time. In contrast, a superior who takes all the credit without acknowledging the team will invite the ire of his subordinates.

Effective leaders create the circumstances for success by assigning the right people, obtaining necessary resources, and providing guidance along the way. Successful execution is the responsibility of subordinates. Therefore, credit for results should flow down from the leader to his subordinates.

Professional sports coaches often provide examples in support of this principle. In post-game interviews, you never see a coach discuss how he won the game. He may have devised the perfect strategy and pulled all the right levers throughout the game. He may have provided all the hope and vision for his players, but he didn't score a single point on the field. His team won because the players performed well. If the coach is an effective leader, he will shower his team with accolades for their accomplishments.

Likewise, regardless of the role your superior had in the outcome of a particular situation, you will invite his ire if you publically outshine him by taking all the credit. You may feel as if you carried all the weight of a given project, and your superior didn't really help you. Therefore, you think you deserve all the credit. Your superior deserves credit too. While you may have provided the direct effort, if the organization you work for has proper accountability, the leaders must answer for nonperformance. Your superior bears this risk. In deference to your superior, you should keep this in mind. Regardless of whether the leadership was poor or the subordinates failed to execute, the top brass usually comes hunting for the person in charge when goals are not met.

Using the sports team analogy again, the star players will usually be deferential to their coach and kick some of the credit up to him or her when their team is successful. The developed leaders among the players know that without effective leadership to focus everyone's effort, success will be impossible to achieve. The bottom line is that you should never upstage your boss.

Don't argue foolishly – When your superior issues a directive, don't openly argue with him unless he is trying to solicit dissenting opinions for the genuine purpose of brainstorming. Hopefully, the superior will have thought through all the implications of his or her directive and carefully considered alternatives, prior to issuing it. If you think the directive will cause problems, go to your superior in private. Express concerns regarding specific portions of the guidance and seek clarification or ask permission to make an alternative recommendation. Make sure he or she knows that you have the best intentions of the team at heart. Deliver your recommendation in the form of question. For example, "Do you think this approach might work?" Another example, "I'm definitely in support of your direction. Do you think if I also did X that it would make the approach even more effective?" Be sure to explain the advantages of your alternative course of action. If your superior doesn't accept your advice, leave it alone unless you think there will be a major catastrophe. Never carry on an argument with your boss. You can't win.

The same rule holds true when your superior is dispensing his wisdom, whether it is truly wise or flawed. Your superior is entitled to exercise leadership by delivering what he believes to be insights. Let him have the last word. When the feedback session is over, calmly consider the guidance you've received and take a break before responding. If his guidance and insight are sound, you've just received a pearl of wisdom. If it is unsound, openly contradicting him will simply be a source of irritation. In contrast, your astute and measured response to his feedback will increase his confidence in you.

Don't catch the boss in an awkward moment – It doesn't matter how well you think you know your superior; you should assume that no one wants to look vulnerable in front of subordinates. Seeing your boss' vulnerability can become a persistent source of awkward interaction. Vulnerability directly diminishes a leader's presence. Here are a few examples to consider.

Let's say you witness your superior receiving an admonition from his manager. The last thing you want to do is ever revisit that awkward moment. You are far better off not mentioning it and moving past the awkward situation quickly.

On the other hand, what if your superior's mother just passed away? Deliver your condolences politely from a distance. Send a card. Don't bring the loss up in person. This will only cause your superior to have to deal with tough emotions in front of you. You may think you're being sympathetic, but the last thing your superior wants is to expose his inner emotions to you. When your superior is in an emotionally vulnerable position, regardless of cause, avoid picking at the wounds.

Last, you should identify the taboo subjects to avoid with your superiors. There is a talent to speaking effectively. There is an even greater talent in restraining the tongue. An example of a taboo subject might be revisiting the conditions that triggered a failed business initiative. Another example might be reminding the boss of a lucrative opportunity he chose to pass up, which is now flourishing. As Benjamin Franklin rightly said:

> *"Remember not only to say the right thing in the right place, but far more difficult still, to leave unsaid the wrong thing at the tempting moment."*

Don't deliver problems; solve them – Leaders have countless problems of their own. The last thing they need is for you to bring them more. This doesn't mean that you should keep problems hidden from your manager. In fact, you should deliver bad news quickly because it rarely gets better with time. However, when you have to tell your manager about a problem, bring a solution to the problem as well. If you don't have a solution to offer yet, tell him that a plan is in the works to provide a solution and that you will be prepared to discuss it by a given time. Delivering problems without solutions makes you look ineffective and less valuable. Instead of bringing problems to your boss, you should offer to take away one of his. Work on a problem that is extremely important to your superior. It's a great way to earn respect and trust.

Speak well of the boss – Have you ever seen a colleague bad-mouth his or her boss publicly? This is the biggest career-truncating move that I see over and over. Some people just can't help themselves. Do they think the manager doesn't have a network in the organization? Organizations are usually filled with sycophants who are all too eager to gossip as a means of getting ahead. I realize that everyone talks about their boss at some point in time. If you feel you must vent about your boss, do it away from the office. Make absolutely sure the person you speak to – preferably someone who doesn't work for your organization – is completely trustworthy. Never spout any criticism in a public forum. In fact, you should speak highly of your superior every chance you get if he rightly deserves praise. Nearly everything you say will get back to him. Why not have positive comments reach his ear?

If you can't speak positively, say nothing. Consistently speaking positively of an ineffective leader will actually make you look like an ineffective leader very quickly. People will think you're not smart enough to identify an ineffective leader when you see one. If you absolutely can't stand your boss, get a new one. You can change jobs whenever you wish. I've seen people actively engage in undermining a superior who they think is ineffective or vulnerable. If you find you just can't support a superior for whatever reason, don't undermine him or no one will respect you. What comes around goes around, and if employees see you behaving this way, they'll undermine you when you are out on a limb. Undermining your superior is not virtuous conduct. If you engage in this negative behavior, you'll only lose the respect of your peers and subordinates. Speak highly of your superior or say nothing. If you just can't stand your boss, leave.

The visible people advance – Arrange for as much face time as possible with your boss' boss. In the final analysis, everyone is concerned about his or her own personal preservation. It's a safe bet that your superior is looking out for his personal preservation. Why shouldn't you look out for yourself as well? Getting to know your manager's boss helps to get you noticed for promotion opportunities. Also, if your superior quits or is let go, having a relationship with leaders more senior than your immediate supervisor will prevent the store of value you've created for yourself over the years from evaporating with your old supervisor's departure. Getting to know your boss' boss is great insurance.

Your Relationship With Your Subordinates

Be approachable, but with limits – The best advice in maintaining a positive relationship with subordinates is to be approachable. If you're feared or too remote, you will become isolated, uninformed, and misunderstood. Still, you don't want to become so open that familiarity sets in to the point where respect is lost. To paraphrase George Washington, as your subordinates' familiarity with you rises, your authority diminishes. When it comes to leadership, the saying, "it's lonely at the top," has stuck for a reason. You cannot become friendly with subordinates and expect to maintain a position of authority over them. In fact, people often deride a leader who tries to become buddies with his subordinates. Subordinates don't need you to be their friend; they need you to lead. They need you to be the visionary, guide, and coach. Trying to be a buddy to your subordinates will only make you appear weak and insecure.

Instead, provide sustainment of the spirit for your employees as often as possible. Check on them and take an interest in their well being. Make certain they're fulfilled at work and are able to grow personally and professionally. Help your subordinates break through obstacles. Listen to them when they are frustrated and push them to achieve results. Rarely socialize with them in a non-professional setting. Professional distance is essential to preserving your role as a leader.

Give credit where credit is due – Publicly praise your subordinates and give credit when a job has been done well. Let your boss know who did the work and pass on kudos to your subordinates in front of your boss if possible. Your subordinates will be grateful for the visibility. In private, be sure that your superiors give you credit for the accomplishment as well. This is not duplicitous. You are not collecting credit for the actual work – that credit belongs to your team. You must collect credit for your leadership in order to justify your existence as a leader, or else your superiors will think of you as expendable.

Set the example – Become a shining example of the behavior you want your subordinates to exhibit. They will reflect your traits, dedication, and drive. Remember, you are the pacesetter. They will follow your example – whether positive or negative.

Relationship Recap

Professional relationships with your superiors and subordinates have a special set of boundaries. Treat your relationship with your superior with silk gloves. Recognize the appropriate ways to interact with your superior:

- Act like you belong when interacting with a superior.
- Play it safe until you understand your superior's degree of leadership effectiveness.
- Make the boss look good and don't argue with him or her foolishly.
- Avoid awkward moments.
- Don't deliver problems. Deliver solutions.
- Speak well of your superior or not at all.
- Remain visible as a strong contributor.

With your subordinates, recognize that they will tend to treat you the way they see you treat your superiors:

- Maintain your personal touch, but keep your distance with your subordinates.
- Their respect for you will be proportionate to how much respect you give them.
- Give credit where credit is due.
- Make sure that all your dealings with your superior set a good example for your subordinates, so they can see that you walk the talk.

Maintaining productive and positive relationships with superiors and subordinates requires delicate balancing. Mastering the nuances is essential to preserve and enhance your presence.

4 Power Thoughts

1. Does your supervisor actively push credit down to you and your peers?
   a. Have you ever been in a situation where your supervisor grabbed all the credit for the success of a task or project?
   b. How did this make you feel?
   c. What do you do when your team succeeds?
2. What did you think of a person who badmouths their supervisor?
3. Have you ever undermined a superior?
   a. Did it work out for you in the long run?
   b. Do you think it's right?
4. Have you ever seen a superior try to be a buddy to his subordinates?
   a. What happened to discipline in that organization or team?

CHAPTER 18

Walk the Talk or Step Aside

"In matters of style, swim with the current; in matters of principle, stand like a rock."

– Thomas Jefferson

L eadership and character are twin brothers. For ethical leadership, you can't separate the two qualities. Character is defined and built by establishing a set of principles and then having the fortitude to live by them. What are principles? Principles are virtue-based values that govern your conduct and the conduct of the organization you lead. In Chapter 15, I emphasized focusing on the establishment of sound principles that make knowing what to do easier. Rules are then naturally derived to align with your principles once the right culture is thriving. That's where the ROLE concept comes from. "Submit invoices by noon on Fridays" is a rule related to the principle of being on time.

Principles are guideposts to live by because they are just and universal. "We will deal with all our customers ethically." "We stand by our word." "I will deal with all my employees fairly, openly, and honestly." These are typical principles found in corporate mission statements.

Your leadership presence is highly dependent upon your subordinates' perception of your character. They want to know your principles. They want to know that you can apply them fairly and consistently with everyone. Subordinates are always watching to

WALK THE TALK OR STEP ASIDE • 157

see if you stand by your principles and enforce rules evenly. Any sign of partiality or playing favorites undercuts their view of you as honest and fair.

Your subordinates want to know that your principles aren't something you cast aside when the going gets tough or you encounter some "gray" situation. Through the process of introspection described in Section I (Poise), you should take a close look at your conscience and the inner voice that tells you what's right and wrong. If that voice isn't loud and clear, you need to work on it. Review the 4 Power Leadership Virtues and practice good habits that reinforce these virtues.

Who Do You See in the Mirror?

Throughout my career, I've faced numerous temptations that could have compromised my principles. Prospective business partners have lured me with gifts. I've been in situations where I've managed multi-million dollar projects with very little oversight and could easily have acted in my own selfish interest. I've had dealings with customers where it would have been easy to short-change them on a delivery when I knew I could get away with it. In examining my 30-plus year career, I live in peace knowing that I've never compromised my principles. The "mirror test" has kept me on the straight and narrow all these years.

The mirror test is very simple – I like being able to look at myself in the mirror and feel comfortable with what I see. I value the importance of a clean conscience in maintaining my leadership poise and projecting my leadership presence. If I feel comfortable with the image looking back at me in the mirror, I know I'm doing my best at maintaining a character of which I can be proud. My father raised me to be a man of honor. He was very "old world," and in his time, honor was a core virtue of his society. If a man lost his honor, he was ostracized. I guess my father's values penetrated my psyche, because I've always fiercely guarded my reputation as an honorable person.

With the right focus, you can achieve a life devoted to living by principles. If you feel lacking in your devotion to virtue, you can make changes to your outlook on life and your behavior will naturally follow. The late Stephen Covey wrote an entire book on this subject called, *Principle Centered Leadership.*

I've found that the more I lead from a position of sound principles both in my personal and work life, the stronger I become as a leader. Your principles are your pillar in a storm. The more you cling to them, the less chance there is of being blown away by the winds of convenience. Abraham Lincoln is one of the greatest leaders in history to underscore this perspective:

> *"I desire so to conduct the affairs of this administration that if at the end... I have lost every other friend on earth, I shall at least have one friend left, and that friend shall be down inside of me. "*

Lincoln was determined to always be true to himself and the principles in which he believed. For the sake of expedience, some associates will often not agree when you take a stand based on sound principles. Lincoln was put to the test many times as president during the tumultuous Civil War years. Even with the immense strains of war and the life and death decisions he constantly faced, he still treated everyone with respect and decency. He maintained his fidelity to his oath of office to support and defend the Constitution. He never wavered in his adherence to his principles. Your trials and mine are not likely to ever equal his. However, we can be inspired by his example. If Lincoln could lead under the pressure he endured without betraying his principles, we can certainly live by our principles and lead effectively.

You're as Strong as Your Work Ethic

Your strong core values must also be accompanied by an equally strong work ethic. A strong work ethic is supported by the virtue of diligence. If you have a passion for what you're doing, you'll find that maintaining a strong work ethic is easy. If you struggle with your work ethic, then you should examine why. Have you always had an issue with how you approach your work, or are you depressed in your current position or career? Your career path is another question worth exploring as part of your inner journey, but rest assured that if you don't exhibit a strong work ethic and commitment to the effort you're trying to lead, your subordinates will know it. Your presence will be undermined.

Set your own personal standard of performance at a level above the norm. Leading by example in this way will pull the organization to perform at a higher level. If you're going to ask your people to go the extra mile, you must always be willing to do so yourself. If you don't care, they will know. As Steve Jobs said,

"Be a yardstick of quality. Some people aren't used to an environment where excellence is expected."

When examining the principle of a strong work ethic, I am reminded of the following biblical passage:

"Whatever you do, work at it with all your heart, as working for the Lord, not for men..."

– Colossians 3:23

This passage is great advice for leaders looking to set an example of diligence and commitment. It can also help subordinates who may be looking for motivation to do a good job on something when their leader is less than inspiring. No one can ever take a good work ethic away from you. A strong work ethic is not only a sound principle, but it is also a marketable skill. Often, it's your reputation for having a good work ethic that sets you apart from the crowd.

You cannot separate true leadership from sound character. If you practice your virtues then living by your principles will be a lot easier.

4 Power Thoughts

1. Do you believe you have a strong conscience?
   a. Can you think of a time when your strong conscience prevented you from violating one of your core principles?
2. Have you ever worked for a person of dubious character?
   a. What was his or her organization like?
3. Write out your personal core values and principles.

CHAPTER 19

Roadblocks to Presence

"We convince by our presence."

– Walt Whitman

"Lead by example" and "Practice what you preach" are time-tested aphorisms. Yet, it's amazing how often leaders fail in these simple requirements of leadership. One of the fastest ways to lose credibility as a leader is to behave in a manner that is inconsistent with what you expect of subordinates. Subordinates are constantly scrutinizing their leaders to detect inconsistency. When they find it, they will not only lose trust in you as a leader, but will also question the validity of your values and principles. A leader's failure to practice what he preaches indicates lack of discipline, and at worst, deliberate and blatant hypocrisy.

Unaddressed Insecurity

Authenticity and the ability to project confidence often fall prey to unaddressed insecurity. Leaders who have not mastered the inner self will tend to exhibit lack of confidence and indecisiveness. As a result, subordinates may interpret what they see as insincerity. A leader's internal conflict interferes with his ability to express his thoughts with accuracy and conviction, thereby inhibiting his ability to manifest his presence effectively. Successfully completing the journey of introspection and establishing your confident inner core cannot be avoided in establishing a strong external presence. There are no shortcuts in this critical step of leadership development.

Acting Before You Know the Facts

Have you ever been in a situation where your manager starts accusing you of having done something improperly without asking for your side of the story? This often happens when a peer makes a complaint, and the second person through the boss' doorway is automatically on the defensive. The inevitable feelings experienced by the accused subordinate are injustice, bias, and lack of trust.

By acting without properly determining facts in advance, the leader damages his presence throughout his organization. Subordinates will look upon this leader as someone who acts in haste, plays favorites, and can be easily deceived. Keep in mind that the first person that comes to you with negative feedback regarding others may have his own agenda and may not always be completely truthful or accurate. In fairness to all your subordinates, you must seek out and corroborate facts to ensure that any dispute or negative feedback is carefully screened to establish the truth to the best of your ability. A common strategy of a manipulator, or the real problem employee, is to put his targets on the defensive by being the first to complain. It's common for bosses to react to a complaint by taking what is said at face value, assuming that it's the truth. To avoid alienating your team during a dispute, establish the facts before acting.

Inconsistent Handling of Situations

Leaders sometimes respond inconsistently when confronted with similar infractions committed by two different subordinates. Sometimes this is a symptom of cronyism. Other times, it is a symptom of having too many rules that are too hard to track and enforce consistently.

If a leader does not maintain professional distance from his subordinates, he may find himself in a tough position when it comes to dispensing discipline and rewards. In general, people like to take care of their friends. A leader must therefore guard against subordinates who will do all they can to gain advantage over their peers by ingratiating themselves with the boss. Don't develop favorites among your staff. The perceived injustice will crush morale. Further, you may repeatedly find yourself in the awkward position of having to enforce rules and policies. If you have too many rules and policies, you may have created a stifling environment. Constantly having to play umpire to enforce rules is not the best use of your time. Also, having to enforce a poorly conceived rule at the expense of high-performing employees will cause you to lose valuable talent.

Subordinates are constantly watching to see if you are consistent in your application of authority. They judge your sense of fairness by how you apply your authority and establish precedent for consistency in your decisions. Set a good example by always being fair, and keep things simple by minimizing the number of rules that your organization must enforce.

Being Too Emotionally Open

Disclosing the inner self to your subordinates is a mistake and not a requirement of authentic leadership. Despite your best efforts to be positive and inspirational, you may have doubts, reservations, and fears. This is normal human emotion that we all experience. Disclosing your inner emotions will make you appear insecure and needy. The well-adjusted leader controls these emotions and replaces them with expressions of confidence, bold action, and optimism. You are absolutely not required to disclose your raw emotions before you have successfully processed them internally.

If you need a release for your negative emotions, seek out confidants who are outside your immediate professional circle and aren't involved in your work. Under these conditions, you can vent your doubts and pain while seeking advice with little fear of repercussion. Everyone needs a sounding board for one's thoughts to help resolve inner conflict. You just can't use any of your subordinates to satisfy this need.

Furthermore, disclosing your inner feelings before you make a decision will only serve to undermine your leadership position. Your subordinates will begin to draw conclusions prematurely before you've completely thought through the proper course of action. By sharing your thoughts too soon, you'll also be creating an opportunity for your detractors to criticize you before you have solidified your supporting logic.

Overwhelming Desire to Control

Great leaders guide and inspire. They minimize the need for personal control by effectively delegating actions and properly empowering subordinates. When a crisis occurs, leaders may react instinctively by jumping in and seizing control. As a situation worsens, the leader seizes more and more control thinking that this will help alleviate the crisis.

Every situation is different and there may certainly be times when a leader must jump to the front and exert control. However, a leader should always be mindful that, as control is centralized, so is decision making. When decision making becomes too centralized, the organization tends to slow down, and its ability to react quickly to changing circumstances is diminished. In addition, when a leader seizes control every time something difficult occurs, what message does he send? Subtly he is saying, "When things are easy, the staff can handle it, but I'm the only one who can do the difficult things." This is very damaging to the morale of your staff and undermines your presence as a confident leader. Balance the need for control and empowerment to maximize your presence among your team.

---

4 Power Thoughts

1. Have you ever worked in a company where the boss played favorites?
   a. What was the morale like?
2. Have you ever worked for a leader that routinely shared his inner fears about situations?
   a. What impact did this have on your confidence in that leader?

CHAPTER 20

Presence Achieved

"The key is to keep company only with people who uplift you, whose presence calls forth your best."

– Epictetus

O nce you've established your presence as a leader, you are able to spread confidence throughout your organization. Your smile and approachability put people at ease. Subordinates feel secure around you; this translates into low turnover and high morale on your team.

You consciously manage the image you project. Your external image is consistent with your poised inner self. You have freed yourself from the debilitating effects of fear. You are a fountain of confidence and project that confidence with ease. Consequently, people willingly put their trust in you. You are now aligned with high values, powerful themes, and sound principles. You are viewed as the spark of inspiration within your organization.

Your confidence and investment in developing subordinates makes you comfortable with exercising minimal control and maximum empowerment. You focus on teaching others to be effective leaders and consistently demonstrate a willingness to listen to others. Your focus is on guiding: not micromanaging.

With the Power of Presence, you are effective at all levels of your organization. The organization views you as someone who can get things done. People do not hesitate in rallying to your call. Your mastery of the subtle dynamics of leadership dialogue reinforces your authority without appearing autocratic. You can appear authoritative without dominating, you don't shy away from tough conversations, and you observe the fundamental rule of leadership dialogue – question and listen.

Through your well-developed Power of Presence, your interpersonal dexterity shines. You have developed the skills necessary to interface productively with your superiors. You have nurtured a productive relationship with your boss. You've become an expert at extending your presence through effective networking. You have mastered the art of the equitable exchange.

Most importantly, you live by unassailable principles and consistently demonstrate the will to stand by them. This is the bedrock of your leadership presence. Now let's examine the power for achieving results. On to the next power – the Power of Performance.

4 Power Thoughts

1. What simple improvements can you make, starting tomorrow, that will give your Power of Presence a boost?

   a. Make a list and work on those improvements daily.

2. Push yourself beyond your comfort zone in taking on leadership responsibilities. You must devote time to leadership for your skills to develop.

Section 3
Performance

CHAPTER 21

Performance: The Third Power

"However beautiful the strategy, you should occasionally look at the results."

– Sir Winston Churchill

There is no dodging the bottom line. Whether at the helm of a business, a military unit, or a non-profit organization, leaders must achieve results. If leadership is about mobilizing people to work toward achieving a common goal, then the measuring stick for effective leadership is clear. Did the organization hit its mark or not? It falls to the leader to accept accountability. He or she must ensure that subordinates understand that accountability is expected of them as well by advancing a culture based on an ownership mentality.

The Power of Performance is achieved when the leader combines the strength of his character with the collective skills required to organize, motivate, inspire, and focus a team toward the desired goals. Performance requires working effectively with people, defining a vision, and generating the excitement necessary to accomplish the desired goals. The leader sustains momentum toward the goal through communication, feedback, and decisiveness in removing obstacles promptly. Let's briefly examine each key element that creates the Power of Performance.

Performance starts with a vision. The leader must be able to visualize, internalize, and describe what success looks like with passion and conviction. He must be able to communicate effectively with his subordinates throughout the organization in order to transmit his vision with power and energy.

A leader achieves results by motivating and working with people throughout an organization. The effective leader is a dedicated student of human nature. He understands what makes people tick and the best tactics to help them reach peak performance.

The effective leader must also possess a thorough understanding of organizational dynamics. In particular, he must have a keen appreciation of the key ingredients required for launching an effective organization, how dynamics change as an organization grows, and the traps that occur when compliance with processes gains supremacy over achieving results.

Effective planning and decision making throughout an organization drive performance. The leader must master the art of effective and timely decision making as well as becoming comfortable with delegating decision making to the lowest possible level in the organization.

Decisiveness keeps a plan on track by resolving issues quickly and maintaining direction for the team. The leader's ability to make decisions for his organization must be supported by the appropriate level of authority that facilitates course corrections in a timely manner.

In planning for success, the effective leader involves subordinates in developing plans for obtaining the desired results; this is a fundamental approach to gaining buy-in from the team. This involvement promotes ownership throughout the organization and is a key ingredient in obtaining superior results.

Information must be delivered to the right people at the right time, throughout control processes, by engaging in sustained and consistent communication. Communication is the task that consumes most of the leader's time during the routine of daily business. Despite all the sophisticated methods for moving information around, communication does not actually occur between people until meaning is conveyed. State-of-the-art communication systems don't actually enhance the transmission of meaning. In fact, conveying meaning is often inhibited by technology. The leader is responsible for the effort required to make sure that an organization is operating based on the same understanding of facts and goals. It can be exhausting on occasion, but it is the leader's ultimate responsibility to make sure that every member of his team is on the same page and communicating effectively with each other.

Having defined the vision and developed a plan that turns vision into reality, the leader must then give attention to promoting teamwork among his subordinates and ensuring that everyone is functioning in roles that best leverage their skills. This includes you, the leader. As mentioned before, you must play to your strengths and design a team with members that complement your strengths and compensate for your weaknesses.

Last, always maintain a profound respect for the value of time. The focused, high-performing leader always maximizes the use of his time and the time of his subordinates.

4 Power Thoughts

1. Think of a time when you were part of a high-performing organization.
   a. Write down at least one great achievement you witnessed.
   b. Why do you think this achievement occurred?
2. Think of a time when you were part of a low-performing organization.
   a. Write down at least one initiative that collapsed.
   b. Why do you think the initiative collapsed?

CHAPTER 22

How to Communicate Your Vision

"Good business leaders create a vision, articulate the vision, passionately own the vision, and relentlessly drive it to completion."

– Jack Welch

C reating a vision for your team is the first step toward achievement of any desired result. The leader must effectively and passionately communicate what success looks like. The vision presents a vivid picture of the Promised Land, enabling your subordinates to visualize the result so they can commit to the overall goal. The vision must be combined with emotion to stimulate the internal desire of your subordinates to believe in its achievability. Vince Lombardi did this most effectively. He was a master at creating a deep sense of belief within his players that they could become winners.

The leader may make a grand entry and impress people with his presence and charisma, but soon, people will demand answers regarding direction. The leadership vision establishes that direction. Without it, the leader will very rapidly lose the confidence of his team.

Visions are bold, grand, and transformative. Visions cause organizations to stretch beyond what is normally thought as possible. Vision is the catalyst in getting people to believe that a desired outcome is achievable. The vision must be sold to your constituency. Belief in the vision cannot be mandated or coerced. Everyone's acceptance of the vision must be genuine, whole-hearted, and must flow from the top all the way down to the lowest rung in the organizational structure.

Sell the Vision

A key aspect of selling the vision to your stakeholders is to clearly articulate "what's in it for me" (WIIFM) for each stakeholder group. The WIIFM can vary from stakeholder to stakeholder, so the leader must look at the world from the perspective of others and determine how all stakeholders can win as part of a particular endeavor. Benefits must be clearly spelled out and personalized for each stakeholder group.

Your vision must also be calibrated over time. Is it still completely valid? Are there new events occurring that require you to adjust your vision? Searching for the answers to these questions is the leader's responsibility. The leader must always be looking on the horizon for game-changing events that must be accounted for. The leader must also take great care in trying to anticipate events. He must factor contingencies into his planning so that tweaks to the vision can be made when necessary. If properly focused and developed, the vision will stand the test of time with only minor adjustments. If the vision is constantly being adjusted or rewritten, then it wasn't an effective vision for the company.

As I mentioned in Chapter 3, when Jack Welch wanted to restructure GE, he set a vision for the company to be number one or number two in each business that GE owned. If GE could not occupy either of those two market positions, the business would either be sold or closed. This was indeed a lofty and ambitious vision. To achieve that vision, it had to be cast as a true "cause" and pursued with a deep emotional commitment. Once the debate and analysis phase was complete, senior leaders who could not emotionally commit to the common cause as expressed in Welch's vision were relieved of their duties or let go from the company. It's all in or out. Half-hearted execution is not a winning strategy. Lombardi followed the same principle. Anyone who was unwilling to accept his vision for the team was welcome to "get the hell out."

For your vision to take hold, it must be founded on common values that are established as key components of your organizational culture. Essentially, the vision says, "This is who we will be in [time period]. We are committed to the following values." The values will establish the support structure for your organizational culture within which the vision can flourish. As we have established, the soundest values are synonymous with virtue, which serves as the foundation for the most positive leadership culture.

Be sure that as the leader you are prepared and able to sustain the environment required for the vision to flourish and become reality. It will take constant communication and establishing a common vocabulary that people will adopt as they discuss organizational goals that support the vision. For the vision to take hold and gain momentum throughout your organization, you must serve as the flame that keeps the fire of your vision burning brightly.

Keep it Pithy

Vision statements are more effective if they are pithy – short, powerful, and easy to memorize. For instance, "Be number one or two in every business we own," is very easy to remember. It can be instantly memorized. It requires no explanation. Let's take a look at some other visions that were set by some of the great leaders I've mentioned earlier:

Abraham Lincoln – Preserve the union so "that government of the people, by the people, for the people, shall not perish from the earth."

George Washington – "The basis of our political system is the right of the people to make and to alter their constitutions of government."

Benjamin Franklin – Enduring vision of freedom and self-sufficiency, "The US Constitution doesn't guarantee happiness, only the pursuit of it. You have to catch up with it yourself."

Mohandas Gandhi – "You must be the change you wish to see in the world."

Steve Jobs – "Make great computers for people to use."

Vince Lombardi – "Be world champions everyday…"

Mother Teresa – "The fruit of silence is prayer. The fruit of prayer is faith. The fruit of faith is love. The fruit of love is service. The fruit of service is peace."

Martin Luther King, Jr. – "I have a dream that one day my four little children will one day live in a nation where they are not judged by the color of their skin, but by the content of their character."

These great leaders all expressed powerful visions that transformed and inspired the people they led. While your authority may only be narrow or you may lead only a few employees, you should still create a vision statement for your team. In fact, developing one will highlight the importance of your team within the context of the greater organization. Capturing the vision for what you want your team to achieve, no matter how great or how small, crystallizes the ultimate goal for everyone.

Let Your Vision Take Root

Develop your vision early on and repeat it continuously. Define it by framing the vision with sound organizational values. Finally, get buy-in from key stakeholders to ensure the vision is perpetuated throughout your organization.

Always remember that your vision will remain a mere dream until you convert it into a concrete and actionable plan. Your subordinates will want to begin hearing how the vision will be implemented or the vision will seem distant and unachievable. Before the excitement of a well-communicated vision evaporates, you must follow up with a plan for implementation of your vision. Involve your subordinates in the development of the details of the plan to increase the chances of acceptance and ownership. (Read Chapter 26 on details for transforming a vision into reality.) Let's now turn to the central focus of leadership.

4 Power Thoughts

1. Research some vision statements that you think are great.
   a. What characteristics do the vision statements share in common?
2. No matter how large or small the mission for your team may be, write a vision statement for your team.
3. Find your company's vision statement. Is it pithy, short, powerful, and easy to memorize?
   a. If it's not pithy, do you think it is having much of a positive affect on culture?

CHAPTER 23

You're in the People Business

"I consider my ability to arouse enthusiasm among my people the greatest asset I posses, and the way to develop the best that is in a person is by appreciation and encouragement."

– Charles Schwab

L eadership is a people business. Undertaking a disciplined, methodical study of human nature will pay huge dividends in developing your leadership skills. In this chapter, I'll cover some key insights into human nature and their relationship to leadership issues.

Leaders have resorted to all kinds of methods to get people to perform, with the most unsophisticated and onerous method being fear and intimidation. Success may be achieved through this approach, but it will be short-lived. Unquestionably, the most enduring success is achieved through inspiring people to give their best.

People give their best when they feel appreciated and know they are making a difference. The inspirational approach to motivation not only achieves short-term objectives, but also establishes a positive legacy for the leader and his organization. To become an expert in inspiring others, you must know what makes people tick. The inspirational approach also requires sustained energy, with the leader working tirelessly to establish a results-driven, success-oriented culture. Inspiring others requires that you first manage your own emotions through the development of poise. Through your presence, you must then convey your positive emotions to those around you.

Devotion to the study of human nature will yield the skills needed to understand the core emotions that drive all human beings. Sustaining high performance depends on your ability to keep people focused and motivated. When you understand human nature, you are able to provide the incentives to encourage high performance and remove the disincentives that inhibit it.

Nothing New Under the Sun

Books on behavioral psychology are good sources when studying human nature, but I have found that researching the lives of past great leaders is also a very productive way to study the subject. The more you read about past leaders, the more you will realize that human nature tends to be relatively constant across the millennia. History is a valuable teacher in showing you how the great leaders of the past responded to challenges throughout the ages. While precise conditions vary, patterns of circumstances do repeat. In this sense, history does repeat itself and therefore can serve as a valuable teacher.

Think for a second about the situations that billions of people have found themselves in since the beginning of time. Undoubtedly, leaders throughout the ages have met some of the same leadership crises you may face today. Why not take advantage of all that learning by reading as much history as possible? The insights you will gain through a committed program of reading history will increase your understanding of human nature exponentially. Read everything you can about great leaders in business, government, and social causes.

Here's an example that might help to understand the value of history. Have you ever had to accomplish something without all the resources you needed? Be thankful that you didn't have to win a war against a well-equipped and far superior army while your resources consisted of untrained, undisciplined, and undersupplied volunteers. Somehow, General Washington succeeded. If you studied what he did, you would learn some tactics that you could apply to your next under-resourced project or your next competition against a larger, more capable company. Washington was able to get people to accept and identify with a higher cause. He succeeded because he knew how to reach people.

Insights from the Great Ones

In studying human nature, I found the insights of America's founding fathers enlightening. Yet, it's easy to dismiss the leaders of the 18th century as less relevant to today's situations. How can we relate to people in funny clothes and powdered wigs? After all, today we are so much more technologically advanced and our issues are different, right?

People like Thomas Jefferson, Benjamin Franklin, John Adams, and James Madison were remarkably astute men who had a profound understanding of human nature. They all possessed extensive libraries and were students of human motivation in their own right. Their study of past power structures in this context led them to design a system of government that would be resistant to the establishment of dictatorship. They studied European history, the ancient Romans, and the ancient Greeks and drew upon this knowledge for their insights in creating a new nation. Their insights into how people behave, given a set of circumstances, were absolutely crucial in framing a constitution that would properly balance power, and minimize the possibility of tyrannical rule and petty squabbles between the states.

In many cases, the Founding Fathers' analyses of human nature approached a foretelling of the future. For example, during the Constitutional Convention, a fervent debate raged on the degree to which the states would acquiesce to a close political and economic union. Franklin, Madison, and Adams maintained that, unless a strong central government was established with the ability to regulate interstate commerce, chaos would eventually take hold. They maintained that relationships between states would deteriorate into constant squabbling over border and trade issues. Each state would take a position of self-interest first, consistent with self-focus. Therefore, interests of individual states would be placed ahead of the interests of the nation.

Today, we can draw a parallel between the debate that formed the United States to the ongoing debate in the Euro Zone. Europe is at a crossroads as it tries to resolve a deep financial crisis. The Euro Zone members have committed to economic union without a strong central political authority. The resulting situation is a stalemate and inability to act decisively to resolve financial issues within member nations. Wealthier Germany is reluctant to bail out the economically weaker Spain at the expense of German citizens. How the situation will be resolved can't be predicted with certainty. It seems logical to assume that they must move to a stronger political union or face deterioration and ultimate disintegration of the Euro Zone. Human nature is constant. Reading history is one of the most expedient methods for gaining valuable leadership insight for current situations.

The Levers of Motivation

Effective leadership is a constant balancing of multiple competing interests in relation to the overriding motive of self-advancement. Now you'll learn the fundamental motivational levers and how to engage with everyone on the most basic emotional level for the utmost in leadership effectiveness.

Napoleon, the ruler who conquered most of Europe in the early 19th century, made a very succinct observation of human nature. He said:

"Men are moved by two levers only, fear and self-interest."

You have to admire Napoleon's ability to reduce a complex problem into very simple terms. Can you think of any motivating factor that does not fall in either of these two buckets – fear or self-interest? Your great challenge as a leader is to gain a thorough understanding of how to interpret and apply the two levers, as Napoleon called them. Let's first address fear.

In modern day corporate leadership, you should focus less on using fear to motivate people and much more on eliminating fear as an obstacle to success. There are many leaders in the corporate world today who lead through fear. "Do what I say or you're fired," is a looming underlying threat in their leadership style. This is a primitive approach and is an indicator of a very insecure and egocentric leader. While the temptation of the short-term success this approach can yield is alluring, it is not a viable long-term leadership approach. When constantly operating under fear, people resort to compliance as their survival mechanism. They will do exactly what you say. They will also withhold their advice and best ideas because short-term survival is no longer based on achievement and innovation. Instead, survival depends on not incurring the ire of the boss.

As long as the leader makes all the right decisions, unquestioning compliance by subordinates will generally achieve the desired results in the short term. However, as soon as the leader errs in judgment and sets the organization on a flawed course, the compliance-driven mentality of his subordinates will deprive him of alternative insights.

Remove Fear

Instead of inducing fear as a tool of leadership, the leader must remain attuned to the various types of internally generated fears that drive human nature and work to remove these fears to the greatest extent possible. The wise leader remains constantly in touch with the emotional state of his subordinates. You'll need to learn to identify the fears that each person is facing when they are struggling. However, directly approaching anyone is not the most effective way to identify someone's fear. People rarely want to admit having any fears at all. Still, through daily observation of someone's behavior and indirect questioning, you can usually quickly identify the type of fear that is affecting someone.

Fear can be tamed by helping people visualize what the worst-case outcome would be if their situation doesn't work out the way they hope. Usually this approach helps people realize that the world will not end and their life will go on, even if the worst does occur. You should explain that the likelihood of the worst case actually happening is remote, because the person can affect the outcome through his or her actions. Finally, you should discuss what could be done so that the outcome can be moved as far as possible toward the desired, best-case outcome. This last step gives people the vision they need to push past their obstacles.

It's worth noting that fear as a beneficial motivator also has its place in the leadership equation, but it should never be your dominant lever. For example, in any business, survival depends on financial success. If the business does not succeed, everyone is out of a job. Going out of business is an underlying omnipresent fear that everyone thinks about from time to time. It's an example of a healthy fear that motivates the organization to compete effectively. However, healthy fear does not immobilize someone from performing effectively, because the fear is not an immediate direct threat. It's a fear that is understood and managed by solid planning and a flourishing success-oriented culture.

Unchecked, fear is the great immobilizer and thief of dreams. As a leader, it is your job to not only control and subdue your own fears, but to encourage your subordinates to let go of their fears as well. Live by the immortal words of Teddy Roosevelt, which I paraphrase here:

> *"...even if you fail, at least fail while daring greatly, so that your place shall never be with those cold and timid souls who know neither victory nor defeat."*

Teach your people to dare greatly!

The Magic Lever

The self-interest lever is the preferred tool in motivating your staff and getting what you want from anyone in your organization. The lever is applied through mastering the art of persuasion. Persuasion is applied by addressing the WIIFM for key stakeholders. The other person's WIIFM is his currency. Currency is defined as what a person hopes to get out of doing a particular task or agreeing to a proposal. Personal currency can take many forms – not just money. Currency can be a simple "thank you," which most often suffices. Gratitude and recognition are often excellent payments and serve as powerful motivators for people to provide service with a smile. Sometimes people have multiple currencies, depending on the situation.

As a leader, you can often satisfy your subordinates' WIIFM by having a ready answer to a key fundamental question from the perspective of the other person – "Why?" Why should something be important to you? Why should you do what I ask right now? Why should you perform to a specific level of quality? Why is this proposal good for you?

When I was an Army lieutenant, I was tasked with organizing a group of young soldiers into a data collection team for the testing of a major Army communication system. A multi-million dollar procurement depended on the outcome of the test. In order to properly staff our testing teams, we drew soldiers from various units across the country. Units typically did not fill our requests by sending their top performers. The troops we were given were not the most motivated. I was faced with the task of motivating these soldiers into doing their jobs right the first time. This was critical because we only had one chance at getting our test right.

I wish I knew back then how powerful the technique I used really was, but as a new leader, I wasn't familiar with motivational strategies. I settled on simply explaining how important their job was and what would happen if they didn't do it right. I told them that the Army was about to spend hundreds of millions of dollars to buy the communication system. I told the troops that this was the last opportunity to test the system under operational field conditions before the fielding decision would be made. I also explained to the troops that if we failed, not only would the Army potentially waste millions of dollars, but that down the road, an ineffective communication system could cost lives in combat. I closed my mini motivational speech by stating that the Army was counting on them to perform the test properly.

Many of these troops were young, junior soldiers who were used to being talked down to and treated as if they were unimportant. It would not surprise me if I was the first person in the Army to ever tell them how important they were to an operation.

The results were outstanding. We had a very successful test, and we had a highly engaged data collection team that often went above and beyond what was required by providing valuable feedback and improvements to our testing process.

I stumbled upon my motivational approach by accident. I naturally gravitated to answering "why," because I would often ask the question when I was tasked with something. Many subordinates desperately want to know the answer to "why," but they're fearful of asking the question. Asking why can be viewed as a challenge to a superior. Therefore, many subordinates do not feel empowered to ask the question. I just assumed that the soldiers would want to know why they were being asked to spend six weeks in the hot Arizona desert sleeping in tents. I didn't know that in answering "why," I was appealing to a powerful inner desire that drives the majority of all human beings – the desire to make a difference.

It was Dwight D. Eisenhower who said:

"Leadership: The art of getting someone else to do something you want done because he wants to do it."

Your powers of persuasion applied through these tools will help you motivate the vast majority of people you encounter. However, there are limits to a leader's ability to motivate others.

In the right situations, a talented leader can motivate a good performer to be a great performer or a great performer to be a top performer. However, a leader is not a personality alchemist. You can't turn employees made of lead into employees made of gold. Chronically unmotivated people need to work on transforming themselves. You can provide inspiration, encouragement, and point the way, but only they can modify their focus and personality traits toward success-oriented thinking.

If you have an unmotivated employee who refuses to join the charge based on your vision, you should not see this situation as a leadership failure. Sometimes, the unmotivated will simply not respond despite your best efforts. Once you've tried your best and given the person a fair opportunity, the best thing to do is cut your losses. Agree to part ways for the good of the rest of your team. Too many low performers will sink your ship.

Master the Human Element

Master the knowledge of human nature, and you will have greater success in getting people to do things. Study the people who report to you. Understand their currencies and what they are looking to achieve in every situation. Align their goals with yours as much as possible. Help others to minimize their fears and become a master of their WIIFMs.

4 Power Thoughts

1. Commit to reading one book per month about great leaders.

   a. Who are the leaders you would like to study and why? Make a list.

2. Can you find any motivation that is not related to either fear or self-interest?

   a. What is your greatest motivation? Why?

3. What is the predominant fear that people suffer from in your organization?

   a. What about you?

CHAPTER 24

How to Know if You're Playing for a Winner

"Even though worker capacity and motivation are destroyed when leaders choose power over productivity, it appears that bosses would rather be in control than have the organization work well."[6]

– Margaret J. Wheatley

O n your journey toward leadership excellence, you should set aside time to conduct a thorough assessment of your organization to determine if it is operating in an effective manner. Doing this is powerful; you will quickly become aware of the typical productive behaviors as well as the dysfunctional ones that can limit an organization's performance. What are the markers that show whether you're working for a great organization?

Assessing Your Organization's Effectiveness

Check the politics first - Politics in an organization is inevitable; a former manager once told me,

"Whenever you have three or more people in a room, there will be politics."

---

[6] "The Irresistible Future of Organizing," Margaret J. Wheatley and Myron Kellner-Rogers (July/August 1996)

When organizational politics goes unchecked, there can be a negative impact on the corporation. Politics can be healthy or unhealthy. Healthy politics is driven by impersonal, nonmalicious reasons such as honest debate over methods and solutions to problems. Unhealthy politics is driven by nonvirtuous reasons such as personal grudges, excessive greed, and accumulation of power for nonproductive personal reasons.

If there is too much focus on internal politics, the organization runs the risk of ignoring the needs of external customers. For businesses, the result would be an adverse impact on its revenues. For nonprofit organizations and government, the result would be waste, inefficiency, or a dissatisfied constituency. Too much unhealthy politics invariably results in a toxic environment that virtually guarantees the decline of an organization.

A closer look at what drives the politics of your organization will help you determine if its state is healthy. To assess the politics of your organization, ask the following questions:

- Are the leader and his staff driving the politics? If so, how?
- Are the leader's relationships with his peers and superiors positive or antagonistic?
- Do the members of the senior leadership team maintain an atmosphere of trust among themselves? Do they care about growing trust throughout the organization?
- Is politics driven by an honest discussion of constructive issues?
- Are cliques and factions prevalent?
- Is personal gain of money and power the predominant driver of behavior instead of organizational success?
- Are there credible mechanisms in place for ideas to be generated and implemented from the bottom up?

- Are people acting more out of fear and concern for their jobs rather than focusing on solving problems and creating return on investment?

Depending on the answers to these key questions, your organization is either managing internal politics well or letting it dominate the culture to the detriment of performance.

Assess the leader - The person at the top of an organization shapes the culture, politics, and processes of the organization. An assessment of organizational politics will reveal a great deal about the leadership. For better or worse, whether intentionally or not, the leader inevitably casts the shadow of his or her personality and perspectives over the organization. Consequently, the organizational personality tends to reflect the leader's preferences. Whenever the leader's personality is focused, committed, and driven to achieve specific results, the organization will also focus on these concerns. If the leader vacillates on priorities, the organization is likely to function in the same ineffective way. If the leader has strong interpersonal skills, the organization will also hold interpersonal contact in high regard and so on. Over time, the entire organization will be molded in the leader's image. Here are some points to consider:

- Does the leader have vision?
- Is he respected by the workforce and in your business community?
- How many of the 4 Power Virtues could you confidently check off in describing him?
- Does he communicate regularly and authentically?
- Is communication clear, consistent, and concise?
- Does he have the competitive drive to overcome the challenges facing the organization?

- Does he have the depth of experience and the background required to lead the organization effectively?
- Does he display an arrogant nature or one committed to learning and evolving?
- Is the leader comfortable with other strong leaders as his direct reports?
- Does the leader surround himself with sycophants?
- Has the leader mastered the art of transmitting his influence, enthusiasm, and vision through others?

Always remember, as the leader goes, so goes the organization.

Evaluate the processes - After you've assessed your organization's political state and leadership caliber, the next assessment should focus on the quality of the organization's processes. While organizations tend to mimic their leader, they also tend to take on a life of their own through a blending of the leader's personality and the mechanical behavior reinforced by the processes instituted by the leader.

As the leader's personality permeates the collective behavior of his organization, he is also usually setting up procedures, processes, and regulations for the organization to follow. Once these rules take hold, people begin to act in accordance with the generally accepted approach and, over time, the "company way" takes over. This can be both positive and negative. Most leaders want predictability in performance. They spend extraordinary amounts of time setting up processes and applying metrics to measure outcomes. They crave repeatability. When results appear to be drifting based on the programmed indicators, leaders want the ability to tweak a process for quick remediation. This part of process implementation is positive. It represents the playbook for the organization; an organization that can reach this kind of efficiency and self-monitoring generally performs well.

However, there's a dark side to overemphasizing process. Over time, the leader may develop a depersonalized view of his organization. As he becomes further removed from how his organization's product is actually produced, the leader may focus excessively on processes and lose focus on the people within the organization. The leader may begin to view his organization as an assembly line blended with his personality. As his attention on process increases, the leader devolves into a simple classic manager and is no longer a leader of people. As the organization grows, an increasing number of rules and reporting requirements are added until a burdensome bureaucracy emerges. The bureaucracy can become so large and demanding that it causes a shift of organizational resources toward satisfying the bureaucracy's requirements instead of satisfying customer requirements. The organization then begins to collapse under its own weight.

Here are some simple questions that can help you determine whether your organization's processes have given rise to a dominating bureaucracy:

- Generally, is it easy to get things done?
- Are the organization's processes simple, easy, effective, and repeatable? (This is the SEER criteria covered in detail in Chapter 26.)
- Do people in the organization understand why they are doing what they are doing, or are they just thoughtlessly following a process?
- Do these processes allow room for thought and input by the people performing them?
- Is the organization driven more by process compliance or results?

- Can processes be easily traced back to the organizational vision and goals?

As a committed leader, you must never forget that all organizations are composed first and foremost of people and secondly of processes. Grow your organization with the human element always in the forefront of your mind. People need nurturing. In a work setting, they need mentorship, praise, and a deep-rooted sense that they are making a difference. Lazy leaders are those who don't emphasize the human touch, lack interpersonal skills, or simply prefer to deal with processes rather than people. They want something that operates like an automated factory so they don't have to use the often exhausting people skills that are actually required of leaders. Instead of teaching and mentoring, they push process and regulations. Instead of building a dynamic culture focused on results, they insist on unquestioning compliance.

You can be far more effective if you adopt and promote great values as the cultural basis and primary focus of your organization. No amount of process can serve as a suitable substitute for enthusiasm. Enthusiasm is only generated through a great culture. This is how great leaders shine, while managers are relegated to counting the beans.

The leader must constantly reinforce organizational values, derived from core virtues, through communication of passion and intensity for the goals and culture of the organization. As Colin Powell once said:

> *"If a leader doesn't convey passion and intensity then there will be no passion and intensity within the organization, and they'll start to fall down and get depressed."*

No one wants to work for a depressed organization that falls down.

Evaluate structural effectiveness - As organizations grow, leaders have to maintain a span of responsibility over an ever-increasing number of people. It's clearly impossible for a leader to maintain direct contact with everyone in the organization. Implementing a hierarchical structure of reporting layers, departments, and business units is an attempt to solve the span of control problem, but it also introduces new complexities. The concept of span of control addresses the maximum number of people with whom a leader can effectively interact without becoming overwhelmed by the communication load. The effective span of control ranges from five to twelve direct reports depending on the intensity of the environment, types of responsibilities, and ability of the direct reports. Examining the layers in the hierarchical organizational structure for some key characteristics will help you assess organizational effectiveness. Here are some points to consider:

- Are the managers of each organizational unit also expected to be leaders?
- Are unit managers sufficiently empowered to facilitate quick decision making?
- Do subordinate managers receive mentorship and leadership training?
- Is senior leadership visible to all the subordinate layers of the organization?

Depending on the complexity of the hierarchical structure in your company, information dissemination can become a challenge. Leaders have to make certain that information shared with direct reports is being properly communicated to lower levels of employees routinely. If it is not, the vision can't be perpetuated and people may also feel left out and isolated. Lack of communication is a catalyst for fertile imaginations. People will begin to imagine all kinds of situations that may or may not be true, because they have been left no choice but to fill in information gaps with assumptions. In well-lead organizations, leaders routinely verify that information is getting out by occasionally spot-checking what employees are hearing. They also hold the appropriate manager accountable if there has been lack of communication.

Check for tribes at war - This next observation is tied to behavior within organizations. People are and always will be tribal creatures. We crave belonging to groups with a specific identity. This tribal mentality can be both productive and hurtful. It can be used to drive esprit de corps within a group, or it can lead to "stove-piping" and artificial divisions within a greater organization. The latter leads to an "us vs. them" mentality that is highly detrimental to achieving the objectives of the greater organization. If allowed to fester, the "us vs. them" mentality becomes one of the main sources of dysfunction within an organization. The leader must be keenly aware of team behavior inside his organization. He must put a stop to any "us vs. them" attitudes that may be developing by reinforcing the objectives of the greater organization. If left unchecked, little "tribes" will form all across an organization.

Look for the curse of the matrix - You should carefully examine the accountability structure of your organization. Any team that is assigned a task to complete must be capable of owning and being accountable for the entire result of a process.

Matrixed teams have become increasingly popular over the years as a means of optimizing financial efficiency of the organization and streamlining management layers. This well-intentioned approach has a detrimental effect on accountability if it is not accompanied with some well-defined formal authority. I call this the curse of the matrix.

In brief, a matrix organization is formed by grouping people of similar skills into individual departments. When someone with a required skill is needed, the department is able to lend the appropriate person to an internal customer. For example, if a company must maintain competency in three specialties, a common practice in a matrixed organization is to place all specialists of Type A in one group, Type B specialists in another group, and Type C specialists in a third group. Each group is typically supervised by a manager who shares the same specialty as the group he oversees.

Matrixed teams are commonly employed in companies that need to staff short projects on a recurring basis. A variety of specialists are assembled in ad-hoc teams for a specific purpose or specialists are loaned to other business units for support.

For example, in the field of federal contracting, the business development (BD) function is often executed by a matrixed team. The BD team assigned to winning a government contract is composed typically of three groups of specialists: account management, capture management, and proposal management. The account manager provides the customer relationship management. The capture manager organizes and implements the strategy for winning the contract. The proposal manager organizes the team to write and produce the proposal.

When a requirement emerges to form an ad-hoc team, the company selects a specialist from each group to form the project team. The individual team members from each specialty group then perform their tasks in assembly-line fashion or as needed throughout the project. At some point during the project, the team of specialists is supposed to have achieved the desired result. However, typically, at the end of the process, no one owns the result! If the result turns out poorly, finger pointing between departments ensues, and the problems are adeptly swept under the carpet. The curse of the matrix rises again!

The reason the matrix approach often fails is the lack of a formal authority chain over the ad-hoc team. It is much more effective to organize your teams so that each team owns the result of the assigned work. The assignment of an individual manager over each of the organizations involved – A, B, and C is often considered proper oversight. In reality, you have three "tribes" who develop rivalries and tensions and none individually feel ownership over the whole resulting product; even though there is a common manager at a level above them.

The better approach is to create integrated teams of A, B, and C specialists who are led by a common team leader who owns the result and has well-defined authority over the specialists assigned to him even if it is on a temporary basis. If the person responsible has no "bite" through formal authority, he will not have sufficient power to ensure the result. The teams can be formed ad hoc, but the leader must be fully empowered with authority over all managerial elements of the team, including the ability to reward, make staffing decisions, set schedules, and exercise financial control. By injecting clear leadership and formal authority, the ad-hoc team and its leader indisputably own the result. Do you see the difference in the human interplay and resulting accountability? By assigning an undisputed leader vested with formal authority, should a team fail to produce the desired result, he and the others on the team are clearly responsible and the team leader is accountable. No one can shirk their responsibility and pass blame to some other department. The matrix approach can be effective and efficient if it is supported by solid processes that provide formal authority to a person who owns the result. Here are some questions you can use to assess this phenomenon:

- Does the organization routinely achieve the desired results by employing a matrix staffing approach?
- Are the results achieved by last minute heroics or good solid team work?
- Does sufficient formal authority consistently accompany responsibility for results?

When outcomes, accountability, and authority are not linked by strong, well-defined organizational procedures, performance is likely to suffer.

Insights for Organizational Leadership

It takes a team to succeed - One of your chief responsibilities as a leader is to cultivate teamwork. That's why I always address groups of both peers and subordinates as "team." I regularly reinforce that the general good of the team must supersede individual benefit. Working in support of each team member is everyone's individual standing mission. Undercutting the efforts of someone else or withholding assistance without good reason can't be tolerated if you're fostering a strong team environment.

When I coached youth baseball, every player wanted to pitch. But in fact, very few players could pitch on day one. There were a few who were capable of learning with a bit of coaching. However, the vast majority just couldn't generate the kind of consistency that the position requires. The good news was that the team needed players to fill eight other positions that were just as important to winning, but required different skills. This is when I would talk with the players and explain that each boy would be assigned to a primary position. I would explain that the most important aspect of their position was making a contribution to winning for the good of the team. The players would generally buy into this approach with little resistance.

Placing each of your employees in the appropriate role is no different in the corporate environment. You have to carefully analyze the skills of each of your employees and assign people to roles where they can be most effective. Know the strengths and weakness of all your people, in addition to knowing your own personal strengths and weaknesses. Shore-up your weaknesses across the team by recruiting complementary assistants, not complimentary assistants.

Once you've got the right players in the right roles, boost their confidence through positive reinforcement whenever they accomplish a mutually agreed upon goal. Providing positive reinforcement when employees work well as a team lets people know that you value their teamwork. Your employees are more likely to continue to act appropriately in the future, because they will want to continue to receive your respect and admiration.

In order to continuously boost the performance capabilities of your team, promote an environment where self-improvement is rewarded. Attach incentives to the attainment of new job-related skills that serve the core mission of your business. Incentives can come in the form of cash, non-monetary awards or promotion. The self-motivated will clearly jump at the opportunity to improve their skills. Those who don't – that says something about them too.

Forming an effective team from scratch - What about that green field situation when you are given an opportunity to form a new team? How do you proceed? I have had numerous opportunities over the course of my career to form new teams for both long-term organizational objectives and short-term, task-oriented requirements. In both cases, my recipe for success is the same. The team needs three ingredients at its core – a visionary, an implementer, and a details manager. These roles represent skill sets more than formal titles. The visionary looks down the road and develops the framework for the plan. He also sets the direction and is the keeper of the goals and ultimate results. The leader of the organization should reserve this role for himself if possible. The organization works more smoothly when the leader is the visionary, because the visionary sets the direction, and the team will naturally look to the leader for that direction.

Next, the role of implementer is vital because this person is key in turning the vision into reality. The implementer must be strong in organizational skills, detailed planning, and delivering results. The implementer will drive the schedule. The role of implementer is similar to the role of the chief operating officer in a major corporation.

Last, the details manager is essential in tracking, reporting, and analyzing performance. This person must be skilled at the use of data and have a strong tolerance for organizing the constant stream of details that flows from daily operations.

Sometimes the leader must share the role of visionary with someone else. For example, the leader may establish the overarching goal, but at times, an additional person is needed to provide the details of the vision. This is common in technology companies where a business-oriented leader shares the role of visionary with a technical leader.

Whether you chose to function as the sole visionary or share the role with someone else, it is still recommended that your team clearly possess all three skill sets – establishing and advancing the vision, implementing the plan, and managing the details.

Master the leadership joystick - As the organization you lead grows or you move up in an existing structure, the additional organizational layers beneath you introduce a new leadership complexity. The complexity arises from estimating the potential downstream impact of decisions you make.

Picture the leader controlling his organization with a joystick. As he nudges the joystick, he affects the whole organization. At layers immediately below the leader, the changes induced by the nudge are seemingly small and inconsequential. However, as the changes permeate downward, the leader's "joystick" can induce chaos, uncertainty, and massive cost.

One example is the "additional reporting requirement." An executive requests an additional piece of information that would be nice to have. He asks that a new report be submitted every week. As the request trickles downward in the organization, the effort to produce the report, consolidate it, and review it at every management layer multiplies exponentially. The costs of producing the report far outweigh its value. This nudge from the leader's "joystick" produces an effect detrimental to the health of the organization, because the organization has now unintentionally shifted its focus from productive work to less productive work. That's why it's important that you thoroughly consider the effects of decisions you make in advance. Assess the impact and determine the value of every new requirement. Communicate and explain change thoroughly and consistently to minimize unintended anxiety resulting from information gaps.

Contain dysfunction - Have you ever worked for an ineffective manager, perhaps someone who is not sensitive at all to the impact of the leadership "joystick?" This situation can be painful, because the dysfunctional boss can cause a great deal of unnecessary work due to poor direction. When a disrupting event occurs, you can be a source of stability. Don't compound chaos by perpetuating dysfunction downward in your organization. You can shield your subordinates by handling requirements at your level or cleverly managing the impact without disrupting critical work your subordinates are performing. Your ability to contain dysfunction from above will be greatly appreciated by your team and will enhance your image as a thoughtful leader.

Master the new media - If you want to rise to the top of a major organization, you must be comfortable with the use of today's communication options. It's becoming increasingly necessary to communicate with dispersed teams across vast geographies and multiple time zones. Learn to take full advantage of all the tools we have available today that allow you to communicate globally, instantly, and on a 24x7 basis.

It is highly advisable that you hold periodic all-hands meetings to address your entire organization, regardless of its size. With streaming video and instant audio conferencing, this can be accomplished with relative ease compared to just ten years ago. However, be forewarned that communicating in front of a group in person is very different from communicating on camera with a dispersed group. The camera is a barrier to human communication and mastering its nuances requires certain skills.

Navigating in the greater organization - Effective leaders learn everything they can about the companies they work for, so they can accomplish their goals. Commit to learning the dynamics of large organizations. Study your particular organization and learn how it works from a procedural and process perspective. Learn how to work the system and learn the functional composition of your organization. Learn the formal as well as the informal network. Remember, in human networks, people that aren't officially connected talk all the time. Knowing this will help you avoid landmines and provide you with important leverage by identifying key allies in the power structure.

A Quick Review of Organizations

Your development and long-term effectiveness as a leader will depend on your ability to understand and manage the dynamics of organizations. Communication, authenticity, and consistency between words and deeds are your greatest assets. Overcoming the common fear of empowering subordinates is the way to increase your chances of success by enlarging your capacity to spread your vision. Learning to spot the talent you need to fill the roles of visionary, implementer, and details manager is key to building a capable core leadership team. The following table provides a summary of the key points to remember about organizations:

Healthy Organizational Dynamics

- Politics is not excessive and doesn't detract from an external focus.
- Processes are effective and reasonably easy to execute.
- Organizational structure is easily manageable.
- There is virtually no organizational infighting.
- Matrix team leaders are fully empowered.

Solid Organizational Leadership

- Results focused leadership with clearly well-developed 4 Powers.
- Organization has a clearly identifiable visionary, implementer, and details manager.
- Leaders understand the impact of the leadership joystick.
- Leaders seldom perpetuate dysfunction.
- Leaders communicate effectively using advanced media.
- Leaders know how to navigate the organization.

4 Power Thoughts

1. Begin a detailed analysis of the organization where you work.
   a. How much does your organization reflect the values and behavior patterns of its leader?
   b. Study all the parts of the organization and identify their value to the greater whole.
2. How would you rate your organization's behavior on a scale from one to five – where five is ineffective and one is effective?
   a. List the top five words that describe your organization's behavior.
3. If you were king for a day, how would improve your organization's behavior?
   a. List the top five changes you would make.

CHAPTER 25

Why Leaders Get the Big Bucks

"Nothing is more difficult, and therefore more precious, than to be able to decide."

– Napoleon Bonaparte

T he root meaning of the word "decide" is fascinating in the context of leadership. The word comes from Latin meaning "to cut off." Cut off from what? When we decide, we consider an array of options and then by selecting one, we cut off all other alternatives. This is the essence of decisiveness. I am not encouraging closed-mindedness. I'm encouraging selection and commitment to a course of action. You need to carefully weigh alternatives prior to deciding. While you may solicit opinions, you must ultimately choose one of the alternatives. This approach is necessary to create the level of commitment and focus necessary for your organization to achieve its objective. Consider this quote to get a true sense of decisiveness and commitment:

"I am sure that if every leader who goes into battle will promise himself that he will come out either a conqueror or a corpse he is sure to win."

– General George S. Patton

Decisiveness is the effectiveness enabler for your organization. A clear decision backed by commitment rallies an organization to success. Once the decision is made, there can be no second-guessing from your subordinates. Everyone must be on board and cannot consciously or unconsciously sabotage the decision, even if they hold a different viewpoint.

Everyone's acceptance of a decision is important, but not at the cost of undermining the leader's authority. As the leader, you should solicit opinions from your subordinates. I encourage you to fiercely debate important decisions. The debate and conflict of ideas is healthy as long as it doesn't become personal. It is also wise to not place yourself in the position of criticizing your subordinates' ideas and alternatives. This will discourage debate and flow of ideas. Instead, encourage your subordinates to debate each other. When someone puts forth an idea, ask what the others think. Draw the best out of your people. If someone disagrees, encourage rebuttal and ask "why?" to drive the conversation. When you disagree with a proposed alternative, don't directly shoot down the idea. Ask a simple question. Refer back to the techniques discussed in Chapter 16.

Sometimes you may have already decided on a course of action. As your leadership experience grows, you will generally know what the right answers are because you will have been in similar situations before. However, it is still better to not impose your decisions on your team. Instead, persuade them to your viewpoint by submitting the proposed decision for debate. Your team will respect you more, and you will likely receive some good ideas.

Napoleon valued decisiveness. For the vast majority of his career as a conqueror, he maintained an aggressive posture against his adversaries by swiftly deciding and moving ahead toward his objectives with lightning speed. When for the first time he failed to decide swiftly regarding a major initiative, his indecision cost him the lives of 600,000 men, his entire Grand Army, and ultimately his dominance over Europe.

His moment of indecision came during his ill-fated invasion of Russia. He lingered in Moscow instead of withdrawing immediately after the Russian army retreated and refused to engage him in open battle. When Napoleon finally did decide to retreat, winter had arrived and his soldiers froze or starved as the enemy decimated them. Thus, Napoleon's indecisiveness sealed his ultimate fate and downfall. Don't let indecisiveness be your undoing.

Frame the Objective

A properly framed objective begins with defining the problem. For example, market conditions, competition, and internal inefficiency have all contributed to eroding margins. Eroding margins jeopardize our existence by threatening our profitability. It's time to decide what to do about it. This is a properly framed problem.

Now you're focused and you're ready to act, right? After all, that's what leaders do. Before proceeding with a solution, there is one critical step that must not be overlooked - clearly defining the objective. Any decision-making process can't possibly work if people don't know what the ultimate desired outcome is. Without a clearly defined objective, it's equivalent to shouting, "Ready, fire, aim!" Of course, it should be, "Ready, *aim*, fire!" This notion may sound obvious, but you would be amazed at how many times leaders demand action without clearly defining the problem or painting a picture of what success should look like.

The "ready" part of the command sequence is your decision process. "Aim" represents your clearly defined objective. "Fire" is your action plan. By extending the previous example of eroding margins as the properly framed problem, a clear objective would be, "We must raise our margin from 5% to 7% within 18 months." This objective is properly defined because it states what you want and includes the timeframe for obtaining it. What and when are the two key characteristics of objectives. "What" without "when" is useless. No momentum or drive is created by an objective that lacks a timeframe. A clearly defined objective, in the form of a desired outcome, lays the foundation for what to do.

Conditions for Deciding are Never Perfect

In many organizations, decisions are stalled because of one major impediment – paralysis by analysis. This is the inability to overcome the belief that you are not ready to decide, because you don't have enough information. Paralysis by analysis is a form of fear of failure and can grind an organization into the ground. It creates outcomes by default. By not selecting a course of action in a timely manner, you are in fact relegating your fate to forces outside your control – your competitors, your customers, and the cold, brutal mathematics of business will decide for you.

It is good to be data-driven because it forces people to focus on facts rather than on what they imagine conditions to be. However, when the data-driven approach is taken to an extreme, you may fall prey to paralysis by analysis. You will consciously have to break out of paralysis by declaring that enough is enough. You will never have all the information you think you need to make a decision foolproof. Even if you do have 100% of the information you want, the success of your decision is not guaranteed, because the minute you've collected all the desired information it becomes obsolete. Information is merely a snapshot in time.

The best decisions are made by mixing information and knowledge with ample amounts of instinct, experience, and faith. It's a careful balance between making decisions off the cuff and becoming immobilized by the fear of not having enough information. Here's an example where I was able to reach this proper balance.

I once worked for a small company that had won a contract to build a video recording system for the Chicago Police Department (CPD). The recording system was needed to fulfill a mandate by the Illinois legislature. The requirement stated that all Illinois law enforcement organizations must record all interviews and interrogations associated with the investigation of murder cases. The purpose was to protect the integrity of investigations as well as the rights of citizens and police officers.

My team began to explore options for designing a recording system that could do the job. We were not a manufacturer, so there was a limit to what we could build ourselves. For example, we were not going to design and build a custom circuit board. However, we considered integrating several components into a single computer frame that would satisfy the requirements of the project. This option would require some work and confidence in our engineers to pull it off. We'll call this the build option.

The competing alternative was to hire another company to provide a pre-integrated digital recording device. Essentially, we would hand over execution of the project to another company. Their device didn't fully comply with what we needed, but the company was making promises that it would modify the component to our satisfaction. We'll call this the buy option.

We had a classic build vs. buy decision to make. My project manager favored the buy option. He liked the idea of outsourcing the work to "experts" and waiting for the desired result to be produced by them. He did not have great confidence in our engineering staff, and the prospect of managing them to produce a result under what he viewed as risky conditions made him uneasy.

I disagreed. I didn't like handing the core of the project over to an outside company. Once we handed over control, that company would then own the intellectual property (IP) that resulted from successful completion. My company would be at a disadvantage in the market. We had to decide which course to take, and the clock was ticking on our delivery schedule. Millions of dollars were at stake, as well as our reputation.

I needed sound information to support my decision. Could we successfully integrate the components to make the system work? Finally, after a few weeks, I had gathered enough input. When I spoke to the lead engineer and asked him directly, "Do you think you can do this?" He responded with a very confident tone, "Absolutely. It's not that big of a deal to me." His confidence struck a chord with me. I decided that we would build the system.

The result was spectacular. We built a highly reliable system that fully satisfied CPD's needs. The project was completed on time and on budget. To his credit, the project manager jumped on board once a decision was made. He was a highly ethical guy who never carried a hidden agenda. We are friends to this day despite my deciding counter to his recommendations.

This situation taught me some valuable lessons in decision making. I collected sufficient information on the alternative. I didn't procrastinate and demand more and more data until I felt risk was reduced to zero. I applied my experience. I knew that putting an outside company in control of a core project deliverable was not a good idea. I had never seen a similar situation in the integration business work out well, and I knew it was important for my company to maintain control over the IP. Finally, I had a good rapport with the lead engineer, and I trusted his judgment. The decision worked out well because I had successfully arrived at a proper mix of information, experience, instinct, and faith. Once we began work, we hit a few snags. The project manager resurfaced his doubts, but I encouraged the team to stay the course and work through the obstacles. This brings me to my next point – make your decisions as quickly as possible and don't change them at the first sign of trouble.

Even if my decision had been wrong, deciding quickly provides an opportunity to recover. Forcing action provides feedback that either validates or invalidates a decision. This is why the military emphasizes decisiveness as a quality to be instilled in its officers. Whenever I'm confronted with a problem, I can still hear my drill sergeant yelling at the top of his lungs during training:

"Make a decision, cadet! Right or wrong, make a decision!"

Indecision is potentially far more damaging than action in any given direction. Action provides feedback while paralysis breeds fear, uncertainty, and ultimate failure.

Fence Straddling Hurts

Fence straddling is particularly debilitating in leadership scenarios because it provides the illusion of decision, when in reality it is far more insidious than even a clearly wrong decision. Fence straddling appears to be a decision because the leader directs action along two courses as a means of hedging his bets. Fence straddling creates many problems. The people executing instructions don't like to work in two directions. They are weighed down by the lack of certainty it creates, and they hate it. As a result, enthusiasm and resources are constantly diluted.

During the American Revolutionary War, there were factions that advocated reconciliation with England. John Adams knew that the nation could not remain divided. We could not support reconciliation while also advocating total separation, and anything in between was detrimental to the nations long-term interests. John Adams eloquently noted:

"The middle way is no way at all. If we finally fail in this great and glorious contest it will be by bewildering ourselves in groping for the middle way."

The middle road is not a decision, though it may feel like one. Rarely are decisions improved by compromising on opposing courses of action. The "how" part of a decision can be adjusted through discussion and compromise. *However, you cannot compromise on two diametrically opposed directions.*

Decide and Act

In making your decisions, be clear, resolute, and conscious of opportunities that will require you to make adjustments. Do not vacillate or consider a complete reversal of your decisions at the first sign of resistance. In summary:

- Once you decide, cut off all other options.
- Get your team to buy in through debate, but recognize that you, as the leader, make the final decision. Decision making by committee is not leadership.
- Make sure you have properly framed the problem and specified the desired outcome with a timeframe.
- Don't succumb to paralysis by analysis. You'll never have 100% of the information you think you need.
- The most effective decision making is achieved by mixing information with instinct, experience, and faith.
- Fence straddling only results in indecisiveness. Fence straddling in decision making is not compromise; it is disaster in the making.

4 Power Thoughts

1. Who was the most decisive leader you've ever worked for?
    a. Was the environment under this leader chaotic or orderly?
2. Do you have difficulty making decisions, or do you make decisions quickly and easily?
    a. If yes, why? Do you have trouble with commitment, or are you too data-driven to feel comfortable with limited information?
    b. Dig deep within yourself and analyze your ability to make decisions.
3. Do you discern facts quickly, or do you recklessly shoot from the hip?

CHAPTER 26

How to Transform Vision into Reality

"Plans are worthless, but planning is indispensable."

– General Dwight Eisenhower

Your thoughts will remain mere dreams until you convert them into a plan. However, as with data, plans are merely a snapshot in time. They are really only our best guess of what we will do in the future. So why plan if plans are worthless? The answer lies in the second half of General Eisenhower's quote – "planning is indispensable."

Forming a plan creates focus. It establishes the objective and the steps needed to achieve the objective within a specific timeframe. Even the best plans can go awry. In the military, they say, "No battle plan ever survives the first shot." As soon as you set your plan in motion, reality will bite you and you will need to adjust. Finally, the most important reason why planning is indispensable – contingencies. If you spend time planning and do a thorough enough job, you should be asking yourself "what if" every step of the way. This thinking prepares you for unexpected events that could potentially derail your plan. By considering the contingencies, you will be able to adapt quickly with alternatives.

At the very least, you will reduce the shock of unpleasant events by having thought of them in advance.

Planning, just like decision making, must be clear and thoroughly communicated to all stakeholders. The plan must delineate detailed tasks and subtasks, timeframes for each task, required resources, and most importantly – identifying the owner.

The Ownership Difference

Ownership is subtly, but profoundly different than responsibility because it conveys a deeper commitment. If you rent the house you live in, you are responsible for it while you rent it. If you own the house you live in, your level of responsibility takes on a completely new perspective and meaning. With ownership, you have skin in the game. Here's a great example of ownership taken from an actual conversation I had with a subordinate:

Aaron comes by my office to deliver some good news.

Aaron: "I decided to go after a new certification. I was really nervous during the test."

Me: "Really. Why?"

Aaron: "The company has stopped reimbursing employees if they don't pass."

Me: "How much are you on the hook for?"

Aaron: "The certification test cost $300. Let me tell you, I was focused!"

Me: "So, did you pass?"

Aaron: "Oh yeah!"

Imagine that! You see how ownership works? Because Aaron had a direct stake in the outcome of his exam, he owned the result. He wasn't merely executing a task. If the company had not made each employee responsible for the cost of failure, he or she would be far less inclined to put forth the maximum effort to pass. Translating ownership to your planning methods, you need to build in the appropriate rewards and penalties to promote ownership. Sometimes, simple peer pressure and a competitive, results-oriented culture within your company will suffice to reinforce ownership. Otherwise, attach personal ratings and financial rewards to successful, on-time completion of tasks. Just make sure each staff member is ready to accept ownership. Any subordinate unwilling to assume ownership will need some counseling.

Build Processes that Work

Plans are targeted toward accomplishment of specific objectives but are often built upon common pre-established processes. For example, there may be pre-established processes for how to purchase computer hardware or how to hire a specialist for a project. Sometimes, the project you're planning may also require the development of new processes. Great processes meet the following criteria: SEER – simple, easy, effective, repeatable.

Simple and easy are two different things. Simple means a process is straightforward, has few dependencies, and few "moving parts." Easy means it doesn't take much effort to execute. The process for dead-lifting 400 pounds is simple. You just bend your knees, reach down, grab the weights, and straighten-up. Simple! It's not easy though. Effective means the process produces the result you want without the need for rework. You can often quickly assess process effectiveness by determining if enough variables in the process are controllable to improve the probability of success. Repeatable is the criteria requiring a process to produce the same effective results every time.

I absolutely detest poorly designed processes that cause us to waste so much time and effort. Often, processes are created with only the needs of the process creator in mind. Consider it your duty as a leader to establish processes for your area of responsibility that meet the SEER test. If they don't meet the SEER criteria, fix them! *Design your processes with the needs of the process user in mind.* If you do, your company will save lots of stress and expense.

Build Feedback Into Your Plan

Monitor progress and look ahead to identify upcoming obstacles by continuously zeroing-in on the next step that must absolutely go right to avoid a major derailment. This is the so-called "long pole in the tent," also known as the critical path. Once identified, focus intently on that one task to make sure it is satisfactorily completed. This approach is a great way to maintain momentum for your plans.

As I've said, sooner or later, even the best-laid plans will hit problems. When your plans hit a snag, don't panic; that's not how a leader behaves. Don't react hastily and implement drastic changes, reversals, or cancellations to your plans. Snags usually do not mean certain failure. There is always a way out of a problem. The naysayers second-guess everything and hurl criticism. The highly motivated team members punch through obstacles and turn problems into success. A well-conceived plan will usually include contingencies, alternatives, and escape routes for risk mitigation. If you invested the time to make a reasonably well-conceived plan, it will likely require adjustments when problems emerge, but not radical overhaul.

As you execute a plan, assume that everything will take longer than projected. Delays will occur when you least expect them. Sometimes, the delays occur because of a lack of a sense of urgency. As a leader, you must become comfortable with generating enthusiasm among your subordinates without alienating them. Normally, all this takes is re-emphasizing the impact of lateness and the cost of failure. Let your staff know that their teammates are counting on them to deliver; otherwise they will ruin everyone else's efforts. Let them know that the reward for success will be theirs. Every team member must share your same level of urgency for specific goals.

Match Authority to Accountability

Responsibility for accomplishment of the plan's goals falls to the leader. You are accountable. You must push your superiors as much as reasonably possible to guarantee that the level of your accountability matches the level of official authority you are given. Being highly accountable but not having authority to implement can be a dangerous scenario. Senior leaders are often too quick to firmly hold the reigns of power while pushing accountability downward. Doing so is illogical, but they still do it.

Authority is your hammer. Everyone in a position of leadership needs a good hammer to get things done. In Chapter 10, I introduced the three types of authority – official authority, implied authority, and perceived authority. Position yourself using all three and speak based on the authority you have. Don't hold back.

No Shortcuts in Planning

If you shortcut the planning process, you deserve the dismal outcome that will result. The achievement of excellent results cannot be separated from the strong forethought required in formulating a concrete plan and executing it faithfully in accordance with sound leadership principles. Plans are the tools that convert ideas into reality.

As the leader, you must be diligent in following the key steps below in order for your plan to be successful:

- Assign ownership of each component of your plan.
- Make sure that all your processes meet the SEER criteria. Sell your plan to superiors and subordinates with enthusiasm and confidence.
- Build in feedback loops and checkpoints to ensure the plan is remaining on track.
- Be ready to attack and resolve all critical path items continuously.
- Expect obstacles and be relentless in moving them out of your way.
- Everything takes longer than you think. Build contingency time into your plan.
- Make sure your level of formal authority matches the level of accountability for results.
- Speak with authority when you are in charge.

Once you are ready to set your plan in motion, you must stimulate desire to succeed among the owners of each component. Use your Power of Presence to create sharp focus for the team. Remember the story in Chapter 23 about the Army privates testing the communication system? Explain why your plan is important. Clarify the impact of failure and explain the reward for success. Stimulate people's enthusiasm for accomplishing the plan by displaying your personal passion for what you're doing. This will create a bond among the team members and help drive their desire for successful completion.

4 Power Thoughts

1. Have you ever reported to a leader who liked to work without detailed planning?
   a. Can you describe the environment that results from the "let's wing it" approach?
2. Describe someone you know who is really good at generating perceived authority.
   a. Describe some of the techniques he or she uses?
3. Have you ever been in a situation where you were accountable but didn't have the right level of formal authority?
   a. What problems did you encounter with your project or initiative?

CHAPTER 27

How to Get What You Need

"It's not what you know. It's who you know."

– Unknown

W ho you know does matter a great deal. Your knowledge alone can only take you so far. Your network is what extends your leadership presence and enhances your Power of Performance. Long-term success requires that you cultivate a robust network throughout your workplace and externally across your industry. Advancing your influence can only be accomplished by seeking help from people who control what you need. Getting things done depends on the leader building strong and productive relationships with superiors, peers, and subordinates.

Early in my career, I had a very naïve view of how people interacted in an organization. Thinking like an engineer, I would look at an organizational chart and assume that only the people who were connected on the organization chart actually "talked" to each other, as if they were wired together on a printed circuit board. By "talking," I don't mean the normal information exchange that occurs during such forums as project meetings and technical design sessions. I'm referring to organizational issues, opinions, planning, posturing, and politics. I was oblivious to the hidden informal organization based entirely on personal alliances, prior associations, nepotism, friendships, and even marriage. This informal organization significantly impacts the way things are done. The subsurface network was the key to how real influence was brought to bear. Over time, I learned that the safest way to deal with someone was to first learn as much as possible about who the individual's friends are.

Creating Solid Connections

Building a strong network requires a major investment of time and should be something you work on daily. Ideally, you should try to add a new contact into your network at least once a week. "Friending" someone on Facebook does not count – neither does establishing a new "connection" on LinkedIn. These types of superficial connections are only valuable if you use them to subsequently create in-person connections that lead to real business relationships.

On the other hand, Internet social networking can be helpful in many ways, or it would not be so popular. Social networking can help you market a product or identify a person you must meet through introduction. You can also use it to analyze who people chose as friends as a way of learning about them. However, when you're trying to create a meaningful business network, meeting in person is critical.

For people to be counted as true members of your network, you must be either emotionally or financially vested in each other. Emotionally vested means you actually care about what happens to each other to some degree. Financially vested means you both have skin in the same game. True members of your network are contacts you've established over time through direct interaction and dialogue. The relationship is cemented through a series of exchanges. People you've worked with, done business with, or rescued in some manner can typically be counted as reliable members of your network. Likewise, people who have rescued you are valuable members of your network as well. Reliable members of your network are people with whom you have mutual trust, because an exchange of some sort has occurred and you both felt positive about the outcome.

Call Them When You Don't Need Them

The time to make friends is before you need something. You begin to create a new network contact through simple exchange of social pleasantries. Take the time to get to know someone on a personal level. Always look for opportunities to help others. Be genuine, or you'll just look like a slimy schmoozer. Eventually, there will come a time when an exchange involving something of value – usually time and effort, property, or money – must occur. If you have an opportunity to provide the first item of value to the other party, do it willingly. You will be establishing good will and have the satisfaction of knowing that you helped someone. The more pragmatic aspect of helping first is that it doesn't hurt if everyone in your network is in your debt in some way. It means you've created a value store with all your contacts. When the time comes for you to ask, hopefully you'll get back a positive response and the help you need.

How the World Turns

You may view this concept of reciprocation and exchange described in the preceding paragraphs as superficial, manipulative, or disingenuous. It only becomes so if you let it. If you are a morally centered and caring person, then your interactions with others will remain centered on principles. You will be naturally pleasant and willing to help others. The resulting strong network is merely a natural byproduct. Most people will want to help you in return if you've helped them in the past. Reciprocation makes the world go round.

Everyone in your company or organization is valuable. The principled leader is not dismissive of anyone, no matter what position they occupy in the organization. He treats everyone with dignity and respect. Often, all it takes is a simple sincere, "Hello, how are you?" to let people know you care. On receiving this simple kindness, most people willingly go the extra mile for you when they know you care about them as human beings.

In the Army, we had a saying, "Be nice to your supply sergeant." The guy who seemed to have the most loathsome, unappreciated job had the power to make or break just about anyone simply by delivering supplies on time or withholding them and making people sweat. He could make your day with something extra or do the bare minimum and make you miserable. Relationships always matter, even in the rank-conscious military.

I've seen managers who are rude and condescending to people low on the corporate ladder, but expect service on demand. I had an acquaintance who never seemed to get his expense reports paid on time. He decided that yelling at the accounts payable clerk was a good idea. I'm sure his paperwork consistently drifted to the bottom of the pile.

Everyone is important enough to be treated with dignity. The practical aspect of keeping as many task enablers on your good side is just one consideration when networking effectively across your company. More importantly, what does lack of courtesy when dealing with a low-ranking individual say about you as a person and a leader? If you only treat important people with respect, those around you will quickly see through you as someone who is insincere. Treat everyone with respect and courtesy across your entire organization and word will spread quickly that you are a positive leader.

Beware the "Net Taker"

If you don't get a yes from those you've helped in the past, one of three things has gone wrong. Either you haven't created a sufficient store of value with the other person, the other person is just oblivious to the game, or you are dealing with a "net taker." The first two situations can be remedied. The "net taker" is someone who is really just a one-way street when it comes to doing favors. These people don't operate by reciprocation, because they always feel a need to derive a net gain from their interactions.

The "net taker" is a negative person who is only interested in advancing himself. One day they may need you. When that day comes, it would not be inappropriate of you to ask that person to reflect on the balance sheet of his relationship with you and with others throughout the organization.

Cast Your Net Far and Wide

In addition to networking within your company, you must also invest sufficient time in networking externally as well. The two most common methods of enlarging your external network are the targeted encounter and the random encounter. The targeted encounter is a deliberate action to meet a specific person. For targeted encounters, the best way to enlarge your network is through the mutual introduction method. Networking is about leveraging relationships. You successively work your way through a chain of contacts, until you eventually receive an introduction to the specific person you want to meet. The mutual introduction is highly effective, because it is based on a chain of trust. The person you want to meet already trusts the person who is introducing you. Because of this trust, the targeted individual is positively predisposed toward you.

Cold calling the specific person you want to meet does not project leadership presence. Leaders generally don't cold call each other; their staff does. If you don't have a staff and you need to meet someone without a direct connection, you can "borrow" an assistant. I've sometimes enlisted the help of a capable administrative assistant who calls the assistant of the person I want to meet. This can be very effective in connecting with someone quickly. Once you meet, it's up to you to bring the appropriate value proposition to your new contact, so he does not feel his time is being wasted.

The chance encounter is an outstanding way to enlarge your network, but you have to be ready with a few basic skills. First, through your newfound poise, you must be comfortable in engaging someone in conversation. Chance encounters can be highly fruitful, because you never know whom you will meet when you are open to meeting new people. Just be ready; the person you need may suddenly appear when you least expect it.

The first thing you should be ready to do is answer the question, "What do you do?" The answer to this question is what sales people have dubbed the "elevator speech." The elevator speech is a pithy and intriguing statement that answers the question and also captures the imagination and attention of the listener. It should entice the listener to want to hear more. Prepare your elevator speech and test it on a few friends. Once you've tweaked it to perfection, rehearse it until you know it cold. Being able to quickly recite it without stammering will help you look poised and confident. When you're in a networking situation such as a cocktail party, a conference, or a business reception, you will quickly be able to stimulate interest in what you do by capturing your listener's imagination.

Now that you are prepared to answer the key question about yourself, you should seek out as much information as possible about the person you are meeting. You should engage in sincere questioning with genuine interest in the other person without delivering the third-degree interrogation. Questioning that is too intense usually produces one of two reactions: "This guy is exhausting me with his questions," and "You are just trying to collect all the information you can." Both reactions lead to a negative disposition.

The best way to engage with your chance encounter is question, listen, agree, and share. Ask a few questions to break the ice and create comfort. Listen intently to the other person's answers by providing feedback. Actively agree wherever you find common ground. Share enough information about yourself to generate familiarity and create a sense of openness, but don't dominate the conversation with a soliloquy about your life. Doing so will make you seem conceited and self-centered, and will have the opposite outcome to what you are actually trying to achieve, which is building trust.

Networking Enhances Performance

The more people you know and can count on, the more you extend your influence. Effective networking not only amplifies your ability to get things done, but it can also be very useful in attracting more subordinates who will want to come work for you based solely on what they hear. Attracting competent subordinates is crucial in building your highly effective team. The strong network you invest in allows you to build your team with confidence, because you are receiving referrals from trusted network sources.

Is it really who you know that matters most? This seems somewhat cynical because it assumes that merely talented people can never advance. The truth is that it takes both talent and a strong network to succeed. Over the course of my career, I have never obtained a job by any means other than networking. Success is achieved through a combination of competence and connections.

Who you know is part of what you know. When you approach professional life – and leadership in particular – with a clear vision of what it takes to succeed, you will quickly realize that cultivating a robust network is an essential component of leadership success.

---

4 Power Thoughts

1. What do you do?
   a. Write an effective elevator speech that piques the interest of the listener by creating curiosity and a "tell me more" response.
2. Do you spend enough time cultivating your network?
   a. Commit to adding at least one person a week to your network.
3. Do you make a focused effort to treat everyone in your office with kindness and respect?
   a. Get to know someone who seems closed and standoffish. They may surprise you.

CHAPTER 28

The One Thing You
Can Never Recover

"Strategy is the art of making use of time and space. I am less concerned about the latter than the former. Space we can recover, lost time never."

– Napoleon Bonaparte

T ime is the most precious commodity you have to trade for economic gain. In business, you give your time to someone in exchange for money or something else of value. The higher your personal value, the more your time commands per hour. When you're a leader, you have the opportunity to multiply your time by transmitting your influence through others. If you squander your time, this waste will be multiplied as well. As the leader, your time commands a premium value because it is continuously applied to maintaining the focus and productivity of your team. The leader's time must be spent on shaping culture, maintaining the vision, and inspiring the team to achieve results in order to extract maximum value from each hour.

Beware of Time Vacuums

Whether they come in the form of people or projects, time vacuums are the distractions that leaders cannot afford in striving for goals. Baltasar Gracián said:

"It is worse to be busy with the trivial than to do nothing."

At least when you're doing nothing, you can rest and recharge your batteries. When you're stuck working on a wasteful effort, you throw away your time and potentially increase your frustration by expending energy needlessly.

Your Subordinates' Time is Important Too

Be respectful of your subordinates' time. Many leaders with unchecked egos expect their people to jump whenever they demand something. You should always weigh the impact of interrupting other people's schedules and plans to insert your requests unexpectedly. Occasionally, something is so important that you must get immediate attention from your subordinates. Use this demand wisely and sparingly. Otherwise, you risk perpetuating chaos downward into your organization.

I've worked for business unit (BU) presidents who routinely receive data calls from the CEO with unrealistic deadlines. The CEO doesn't realize that his inability to maintain an orderly time management routine causes the BU president to divert his attention from the important tasks he's doing. The division president feels compelled to devote his attention to the CEO's request. He therefore rearranges his schedule, cancels meetings, and is not present for critical reviews of important projects. His subordinates are delayed in receiving guidance and obtaining decisions. The BU

234 • 4 POWER LEADERSHIP

president must then request assistance to satisfy the data call. He turns to one of his direct reports and delegates parts of the CEO's request to him. The direct report in turn assigns parts to three other subordinates who must now all stop what they were working on. Do you see the ripple effect that poor time management causes? If this scenario is repeated often enough, your bottom line will take a hit and your competition will gain market share because of your company's disordered management style.

Feel empowered to push back against ridiculous deadlines imposed from above. Of course, do this respectfully. Remember the potentially fragile ego of the individual above you. I once received a request from my boss to "rearrange my schedule for tomorrow" so that I could attend a meeting he was trying to schedule. The meeting was definitely important to him, but it needed to be weighed against what I was doing from the perspective of the greater value to the company. I gently pushed back by telling him about the importance of the meetings that I had already scheduled. I simply asked him if the urgency of his request outweighed what I was doing. Most reasonable people acquiesce to this sort of logic. An individual who is eager to please his boss at all costs would have simply said yes. You could make a case that he's being politically savvy. But in fact, this person isn't acting in the company's best interest, because he isn't applying his time to tasks of greater value in the right sequence. If you properly manage your relationship with your superiors, in most cases they will be flexible and understanding.

Your life is like a candle with time being the wick. Whether you're on the job or on personal time, don't burn your wick on worthless pursuits. Your life is always a direct result of how wisely you used your time. Once the wick is burned, it is gone forever.

4 Power Thoughts

1. Does your organization constantly react to last-minute requests from executives?

   a. How does this impact morale?

2. If you were lying on your deathbed, what would stand out as the time you wish you could reclaim?

   a. Why do you spend time on this activity?

3. Identify a time vacuum in your personal life that affects you the most.

   a. Consider the impact of the lost time on your career.

   b. Consider the impact on your relationships with people who are dear to you.

CHAPTER 29

Roadblocks to Successful Performance

"It's no use saying, 'We are doing our best.' You have got to succeed in doing what is necessary."

– *Winston Churchill*

L eaders are responsible for delivering results. Yet, they may unwittingly undermine their own organization's ability to perform. On the following pages, you will learn how to identify common patterns of self-defeating behavior.

Failure to Create a Winning Environment

Leaders must create the environment in which personnel can thrive and achieve the required results. Unless they properly think through their plans, organizational structures, and incentive programs, leaders can unwittingly become inhibiters of the effective organizational performance they are trying to create. Formal performance evaluation systems must be properly designed to ensure that employees are incentivized to excel. Leaders should strive to recognize top performers and identify poor performers.

In an effort to do this, some companies have at times used fixed allocation rating systems to rank employee performance. Here's how this type of system works: regardless of individual competence, managers are allocated a fixed number of top ratings, mid-ratings, and poor ratings. For example, if a manager oversees ten employees, he is compelled by the system to give three top ratings, six mid-ratings, and one low rating. Seems logical until productivity crashes.

The employees who feel most slighted and leave are the mid-tier performers who were not able to receive a top rating, but felt they deserved one. These are the performers who are on the rise, but may have just missed a top rating. The valuable mid-tier employees often quit so they can move on to a company that treats them as top performers. Also, the system doesn't actually eliminate poor performers who have few job options, unless management actively pursues firing them.

The policy example above is intended to improve the quality of the overall workforce by weeding out low performers. However, it has unintended consequences because the leaders ignored the "human" in human resource management. People react based on incentives of reward or punishment. They react to forces that threaten their safety as a means of resolving their fear and self-interest. When employees determine that their ranking against their peers could threaten their jobs, their behavior immediately shifts to competing against their peers instead of focusing on the real competition – rival companies. The resulting internal rivalries prove detrimental to the company's performance and hurt its ability to retain excellent mid-level performers. Management has inadvertently created an environment that inhibits positive outcomes – exactly the opposite of their intent.

In your leadership role, you may not have the authority to reverse ineffective policies such as fixed allocation rating. Such policies are often dictated from the top of the corporation. However, there are two things you can do. First, you can engage your creativity in tapping alternative currencies as rewards for mid-tier performers. The formal rating system may prevent you from delivering monetary rewards, but you can use rewards such as training, conference attendance, and other perks as ways to assuage the battered feelings of valuable subordinates. Second, you can collect data on the impact of the rating system on employees. Present this data to management in a well-reasoned and constructive context. You can use your analysis to stand out as a leader.

Failure to Empower Key Subordinates

In today's lightning-fast economy, organizations must be nimble. Large companies must execute with the speed of small business or risk losing market share to their competitors. Minimizing bureaucracy and making decisions at the lowest possible level achieves organizational speed. Leaders often do not strike the right balance between decisions they absolutely must make and decisions that can be delegated. This creates a tendency to consolidate decision making upwards instead of distributing it downwards. The illusion of control gives leaders a sense of power, but is actually harmful to the overall health of their organization. As decisions are consolidated upwards, the organization slows down. Senior decision-makers get bogged down as their calendars become increasingly jammed with meetings requested by subordinates for the sole purpose of extracting decisions. The delay caused by this type of environment is costly. Subordinates are not empowered to complete anything independently, thereby creating a central bottleneck among the few leaders authorized to make decisions.

Last-Minute Interjection

The organization suffering from low empowerment will become increasingly dysfunctional due to an increase in last-minute arrival of senior management guidance. When empowerment is low, the burden on senior leaders increases. Their schedules become busier and they are unavailable at critical moments to provide guidance to subordinates. Invariably, subordinates will do the best they can in the absence of guidance, only to receive last-minute interjection from senior leaders regarding previously unaddressed issues. This symptom results directly from a failure to devote sufficient leadership time and attention early in a process and the lack of empowerment of subordinates. When leaders get involved at the last minute, they become risk averse, creating a desire to constantly hedge their positions. This further undermines performance by adding cost to reanalyze decision points that the staff has already processed and moved beyond.

The Defensive Mentality

Have you ever worked for someone who was always playing defense? Did that feel like a winning posture in your business pursuits? Playing defense doesn't win business and doesn't grow companies. A solid plan with a willingness to accept prudent risk generates growth. When leaders don't empower subordinates, the environment becomes distrustful. Subordinates punt everything upstairs, and because leaders feel uncomfortable with the small amount of time they've spent on a given problem, they can't feel committed to the decisions they are required to make. This leads to a defensive mentality where leaders fuel the bureaucracy by demanding additional documentation, conducting excessive review, and second-guessing subordinates because of their own uncertainty and lack of faith in their own organization's ability.

Obstructer or Enabler?

Have you ever worked for a naysayer? How debilitating is it to work for someone whose sole function seems to be to blast holes in your work and action plans? The naysayer consistently refuses, opposes, finds fault with, and is skeptical or cynical about nearly every decision, policy, plan, or recommendation. He rarely works to resolve an issue. This type of behavior may seem like a variation of the defensive mentality, but it actually goes deeper. Being a naysayer is an actual personality trait and not just a conditioned response within the work environment. The naysayer has a negative approach to life in general. In a leadership position, the naysayer is quick to identify obstacles but rarely proactively recommends solutions. Real leaders inspire. They teach others that no obstacle is too big. The naysayer in a leadership position unknowingly stamps out inspiration by constantly focusing attention on everything that could go wrong.

4 Power Thoughts

1. Identify leadership behaviors and practices in your organization that are obstacles to performance.
   a. What is the source of these obstacles?
   b. What kinds of impacts do these behaviors and practices cause?
2. Identify the range of decisions your boss routinely makes.
   a. How many of these decisions do you feel that you or a peer could handle instead?

CHAPTER 30

Performance Achieved

"I never shall shine 'til some animating occasion calls forth all my powers."

– John Adams

L eaders arise from some of the most unexpected circumstances; we just don't know what we are capable of until we are tested. Leaders rise to the challenge in a time of crisis because they spend time making themselves ready for the opportunity to lead.

Where was General Patton before entering combat in World War II? He was sweating in the blistering heat of the California desert about 50 miles southeast of Palm Springs, training his army in conditions that resembled what they were about to face in North Africa. Coming from a long line of military leaders in his family, he certainly had several role models to emulate. He knew that relentless preparation was the only way to succeed. He studied history, and more importantly, he studied his enemies. He built a complete mental picture of the terrain, conditions, and psychology of the enemy. He was compelled to succeed at his job, because the lives of his men depended on him being prepared to shoulder the responsibilities he was about to be handed.

Patton possessed all the powers, traits, and skills of leadership that I've covered so far. He was totally self-aware of his capabilities as a leader. He possessed supreme inner confidence and was extremely skillful in projecting that confidence to establish his presence as a leader. Patton knew how to deliver results. He was a master of the Power of Performance.

Patton was demanding and tough, but even the soldiers and direct subordinates who may have secretly disliked him would rather fight for him than any other general. Subordinates felt the same way about Steve Jobs, Jack Welch, and Vince Lombardi. These leaders proved repeatedly that they delivered results, and everyone wants to work for a winner.

Similarly, Patton's direct reports knew that he would develop a vision for success and was adept at getting them to believe in themselves and the outcome of his vision. Patton was a meticulous planner who knew how to organize his resources for maximum effect. He was decisive and always willing to take bold action with lightning speed while not ever crossing the line into recklessness. Despite the calculated risks, Patton committed to a decision and stuck with his plans.

All of Patton's heritage, training, preparation, and experience came to a climax in his final days as a combat general. During the period from entrance of his Third Army into combat after the Normandy invasion to conclusion of the war in Europe, his army achieved astounding successes. Here is an excerpt detailing his army's accomplishments in Patton's own words: [7]

> "During the 281 days of incessant and victorious combat, your penetrations have advanced farther in less time than any other army in history. You have fought your way across 24 major rivers and innumerable lesser streams. You have liberated or conquered more than 82,000 square miles of territory, including 1500 cities and towns, and some 12,000 inhabited places. Prior to the termination of active hostilities, you had captured in battle 956,000 enemy soldiers and killed or wounded at least 500,000 others."

---

[7] General George S. Patton - General Orders (Number 98) issued May 9, 1945

The Power of Performance is the power to produce results. Results are the indisputable product of leadership. Master the following key points for developing your Power of Performance and your ability to deliver results will soar:

- Develop and promote a vision. Paint a picture of what success looks like.
- Motivate others through management of rewards, removal of fear, and appealing to self-interest.
- Master organizational dynamics and learn how to cure dysfunctional teams.
- Exercise being decisive. Don't allow yourself to be paralyzed by the fear of not having enough information.
- Build plans that achieve results and drive completion through accountability and ownership culture.
- Time is half of what you have to trade. The other half is knowledge. Use your time wisely and remain focused on continuously boosting your knowledge.

Preparation for leadership is a lifelong process of committed study and personal trial. Commit today to becoming the best possible leader you can be. Read every book you can on leadership. Store the knowledge you've acquired, knowing that one day you will be called to lead. There will come a time when all your powers – Poise, Presence, and Performance wrapped in one last power, the Power of Persistence, will be needed.

4 Power Thoughts

1. Which one of your favorite leaders demonstrated an out-standing ability to achieve results?

   a. To what qualities do you attribute his or her success?

2. Do you personally know someone who is excellent at achieving results?

3. What quality do they possess that you credit most for their success?

Section 4
Persistence

CHAPTER 31

Persistence: The Fourth Power

"Victory belongs to the one persevering."

– Napoleon Bonaparte

P ersistence is the pervasive power of leadership. It is the fuel that propels the leader forward. To attain poise, you must work, just as you must work to become skilled at projecting presence and mastering the art of achieving results – performance. Anything that requires work is met with resistance. There is only one way to overcome resistance – persistence.

Now let's look at the Power of Persistence from the perspective of achieving goals. Often, the difference between success and lack of achievement is simply "getting in the game." There are many people with mediocre talent who are achieving success every day because they are simply pushing ahead with their goals. They are in the game and playing hard. What they may lack in talent, they make up in persistence. Compare these individuals to highly capable people who possess all the required mental faculties and talent but lack just one quality – the persistence to get in the game and to keep showing up, no matter what comes against them.

The leader who has mastered the Power of Persistence views goals as non-negotiable. When you want to achieve something, you must approach your goal with a clear-headed and unshakeable resolve that you will achieve your aims with or without assistance of so-called gatekeepers. You will go over or under, around, or through any obstacle. No is not an option. *The determined leader starts with yes and focuses thinking on how.*

Let's say you've worked hard and developed the traits and behaviors you need to be a successful leader. You assume a leadership position in an organization. You develop a vision and begin to set goals for turning that vision into reality. Suddenly, setbacks begin to occur. Some staff members will give in to doubt and fear at the first signs of trouble and become paralyzed. This behavior of arriving at the first obstacle and stopping resembles the behavior of livestock. They are often contained in a pasture by a flimsy barbed-wire fence. Because the wire represents some short-term pain, the animal doesn't challenge it. He is not aware of his own strength and that, with a bit of effort, he could probably push right through the fence.

When an organization is not empowered by its leadership and inspiration is low, people tend to be reticent in tackling challenges they encounter. It can be frustrating as they repeatedly reach an obstacle and stop. It's your job as the leader to assert your Power of Persistence and inspire your staff through encouragement, brainstorming of options, and sometimes a metaphorical "kick in the pants" as a last resort to generate action. You must steel your organization to withstand the trepidation that results from encountering obstacles. By all means, equip people with the tools and authority they need to succeed.

4 Power Thoughts

1. Have you had an experience where you gave up on a goal only to find out that if you had persisted just a bit further, success was around the next corner?
2. What would you do differently?
3. Conversely, have you ever pursued a goal so fervently that nothing could stop you?
4. What was the difference between the two situations?

CHAPTER 32

Your Hidden Fuel

"My great concern is not whether you have failed, but whether you are content with your failure."

– Abraham Lincoln

L eaders are simply not permitted to dwell on failure. An empowering attitude that enables you to properly deal with failure is key to establishing the Power of Persistence. When you encounter failure, you can surrender to it and make it permanent, or you can learn a hard lesson and charge right back into the game for another chance.

Failure is fuel for your engine. Put it in your tank and move on. Immediately learn from the failure, extract the positives, and quickly dispose of the negative emotions to avoid souring your attitude.

Relish Your Victories; Banish Your Failures

Dwelling on your failures is wasted energy. The mind is always ready to lavish pain on us as an obscene reward for our failings. Unless you stop the process, when confronted with a new challenging situation, our mind will quickly dredge up all those scenarios stored away in our brains that meticulously catalogue all the times we failed. It's vitally important that we not play these bad movies in our heads. Instead, develop a reel of your victories.

Feel free to play those movies as often as you wish. Relish and leverage your victories. Always use them as testimonials and reminders that you know how to win, but more importantly that you have the will to win.

Leaders are Relentless and Irrepressible

Failure can be your greatest teacher. I made the point earlier that action provides instant feedback. When things are proceeding as we intended, it's easy to think that all is well, until we realize that what we intended is actually not what we needed. Failure shapes our course of action until the ultimate success is achieved. Failure is a result that can be evaluated. In his book, *Awaken the Giant Within*, Tony Robbins makes the point:

"There are no failures in life. There are only results."

Failure is merely a name we use for a result we didn't want. While this thinking may be viewed as playing with semantics, the point is well-made. You are free to change the results you're getting anytime you want by conducting another trial and by reengaging in the great game of life. You can choose whether to make failure permanent.

When it comes to overcoming failure, I have two favorite words that always come to mind: *relentless* and *irrepressible*. Relentless captures perfectly the thought of sustained, unstoppable, and dogged effort in the pursuit of one's goals. Irrepressible is the perfect expression for effort that cannot be restrained when a clearly defined goal is burning in our hearts.

Stay on Offense

We can look to a rising star in the golf world for contemporary inspiration on how failure, properly channeled, can ultimately lead to great success. In 2011, Irishman Rory McIlroy, at just 21 years old, led The Masters by four strokes heading into the final round, only to watch his lead evaporate in a crushing collapse, which included a triple bogey on the 10th hole. As shot after shot went awry, his powers of concentration shifted from swinging his club perfectly to merely containing his tears as one of golf's most coveted championships slipped through his fingers.

Meanwhile, Carl Schwartzel, a 27-year-old South African player, was playing offense. He had nothing to lose at the start of the final round. This freed him to play aggressively. Schwartzel birdied his final four holes and captured the championship.

A person of weaker character might have let the epic collapse viewed by millions on a world stage destroy his confidence. Instead, McIlroy chose to learn from his spectacular failure. On that fateful day, McIlroy was thinking of not making mistakes instead of playing a relaxed, aggressive style as he always had before. The self-generated internal tension was his undoing. Having learned from his failure, two months later, Rory roared back. He won the U.S. Open by eight strokes!

Rory McIlroy's story has great hidden lessons in it for everyone. Once we achieve a certain level of success, we may become protective of our position. We suddenly stop doing what has worked and begin playing defense. We shift our focus from growth to maintenance. As McIlroy entered the final round, he must have been thinking about what not to do: "Don't make critical mistakes. Just hit the fairways and the center of the green." After all, he had a good lead. He didn't necessarily need to grow that lead – just maintain it.

In business, we can easily arrive at the same mentality. Our early efforts that created sharp focus and energy in pursuit of our goals can become blunted once we start to achieve success. Suddenly, we start thinking of maintaining our comfortable position instead of growing. Before too long, we'll find that our competitors have overtaken us. Business is chock full of such stories – Kodak, Xerox, and Sears are prime examples of companies that are mere shells of what they once were. These companies played defense when their competitors were busy striking at the heart of their business.

When leading the game, don't play defense; stay on offense. Your competitors are hunting for you. If you encounter failure, master its lessons quickly so you can right your ship before it's too late. Once you've drawn all the positive learning from failure, put it behind you permanently.

4 Power Thoughts

1. Do you still feel haunted by a past failure?
    a. Think of ways you can put it in the proper perspective.
    b. Extract the important lessons you can apply for the future. Learn and move on.
2. Have you ever worked in an environment that is gripped by fear of failure? Describe the interpersonal relationships in this environment.
3. Conversely, have you ever worked in a positive, can-do environment where experimentation is encouraged and failure is a learning opportunity? Describe the interpersonal relationships in this environment.

CHAPTER 33

How to Get the Glory

"Courage is the first of human qualities because it is the quality which guarantees all the others."

– Winston Churchill

C ourage is the quality that enables persistence. A leader's ability to persevere is undermined if he does not have a well of strength within him when challenges arise. The well of strength is found in virtue.

Courage is a Foundational Virtue

Many soldiers demonstrate the ultimate form of courage on the field of battle. With their lives at stake, they find the inner strength to perform their duty. When asked how they persevere, the most common answer is, "I'm just doing my job." This is actually a humble reply that masks the drive behind their performance. That drive is derived from a firm footing in the virtues of honor and loyalty. They are rooted in honor because they swore an oath to defend the country, and they are rooted in loyalty, not only to their country, but to their fellow soldiers. When the shooting starts, they simply "do their jobs" because people are depending on them.

Fortunately, in the corporate world, no one is shooting at us. In the end, it's just business. This thought alone should be a source of strength because it lends perspective. We often make more of our challenges in business than they really are. Most of the time, we act like everything is a matter of life and death. In reality, the worst we may suffer is a bit of humiliation. That may be ego death, but it's not real death.

The relative comparison of the courage it takes to act in the face of physical danger versus the courage required to lead in the corporate world, should have a grounding effect on business leaders. Yet, I often see ineffective executives approach the most basic decisions with trepidation instead of courage. Rarely do the day-to-day decisions made by a corporate leader require the type of courage that even remotely compares to courage required on the field of battle. If you find yourself faced with a tough decision requiring you to summon your courage, lighten up and get some perspective.

The courage of the most senior corporate leaders is often tested by circumstances requiring decisions on strategic courses of action that bear significant monetary risk. For leaders at the top of the corporate pyramid, the stakes can be extremely high and the pressure intense. They must summon the courage to make decisions with impacts ranging into billions of dollars. In extreme circumstances, corporate survival can also be at stake when a major crossroad is encountered regarding business strategy. Competitive challenges must be confronted with bold action. When a business heads into a downturn, will the leader in charge have the courage to swiftly decide which course to take?

Depending on your current leadership level within your organization, you may not be faced with any of these tests of courage in the near future. However, there is one common test of courage that seems to touch all leaders, regardless of their level or where they work. The test is having courage to stick to virtues at all costs. This is courage of the spirit.

The Moral High Ground Takes Courage

When a leader encounters a difficult situation in which he must choose to either uphold his values or ignore them for the sake of expediency, his courage of the spirit will be tested.

The greatest leaders of all time consistently demonstrated their courage of the spirit. Lincoln, Gandhi, King, and Washington, as a few examples, all stood tall when it came to defending their principles. In business, politics, and religion, we can unfortunately find many examples where leaders chose expediency over virtue by covering up wrongdoing. Their courage of the spirit was clearly lacking or nonexistent.

A leader's character is shaped by his willingness to stand up for his values. Like all leadership qualities, courage of the spirit can be nurtured. It starts by acknowledging our common human virtues that form our character. You can strengthen your courage of the spirit by doing simple things such as telling the truth even when you know there will be consequences, because truth is a virtue that is not worth sacrificing to hide a problem or mistake. Another good example is justice. When one person commits a transgression, the consequences should be the same for all.

Standing for your principles may cost you in the short run. However, losing yourself through a bad decision is far more costly. Ultimately, you will find that leaders who display great courage of the spirit will be able to navigate through their business trials more easily. Here is a remarkable example of effective leadership.

During the great recession of 2008, steelmaker Nucor did not lay off a single worker. Long before the recession hit, their management, led by CEO Dan DiMicco, had devised a compensation system where workers' pay was tied to productivity. During strong business cycles, they would be very well compensated.

During poor business cycles, their incentive pay would go down due to low production, but their jobs would not be cut.

Given the severity of the recession, Nucor could easily have claimed extraordinary circumstances as a reason for a mass layoff. Instead, the company demonstrated extraordinary loyalty to its workers during difficult economic times. Because Mr. DiMicco and his management team had the courage to make such a difficult economic decision, they now have one of the most grateful, motivated, and loyal work forces in the steel industry. Nucor management had the courage to stand by its values.[8] In the words of Baltasar Gracián:

> *"Wisdom backed by courage makes greatness."*

Courageous and ethical leadership can indeed exist in organizations. When leaders profess high virtue and then treat subordinates in a manner consistent with the virtues they profess, subordinates return motivation, loyalty, and outstanding results. Trust in their leader soars because he or she has successfully "walked the talk."

In the leadership philosophy of Vince Lombardi, courage requires "mental toughness." Coach Lombardi was a proponent of a solid value system as a foundation for all greatness. Courage was at the top of his list. This is how the great coach viewed mental toughness and courage:

> *"Mental toughness is many things and rather difficult to explain. Its qualities are sacrifice and self-denial. Also, most importantly, it is combined with a perfectly disciplined will that refuses to give in. It's a state of mind—you could call it character in action."*

---

[8] In the interest of full disclosure, I do own some Nucor stock. I bought it after I heard the story I just recounted.

Courage is fortified by occupying the moral high ground. There is great strength in knowing that your stand has the power of moral authority behind it. Abraham Lincoln summarized this point perfectly:

"Be sure you put your feet in the right place, then stand firm."

Sometimes the moral high ground and the expedient or technically correct position will be in conflict. That's why as a leader you must exercise your courage to make the best decisions possible. The moral high ground always has a greater long-term return on investment.

Courage is the Antidote to Fear

Conquering fear of failure should be your number one priority in bolstering your Power of Persistence and enhancing your Power of Presence. Courage doesn't mean we are never afraid or anxious, but the Power of Persistence is what we engage as leaders to make sure fear doesn't stop us.

In the face of business challenges, your subordinates will examine your demeanor. If you are calm, confident, and courageous, they will be too. Having planned effectively and selected the right people to execute your plans, expressions of faith in your team can clinch the deal on boosting courage across your organization. A deep sense of faith in your ability to find your way through a problem will provide the grounding you need.

4 Power Thoughts

1. Think of an example where you have observed courage in leadership.
   a. How was the situation in your example driven by strong values?
2. Would you sacrifice your values in favor of self-interest?
   a. We may all be quick to answer no, but have you been tested?
   b. Are your values deeply rooted in your personality?

CHAPTER 34

Roadblocks to Persistence

"Success seems to be largely a matter of hanging on after others have let go."

— *William Feather*

F or the uncommitted, persistence can evaporate at the first sign of resistance and goals can be easily abandoned. People who exhibit this behavior were probably never deeply committed to the goal in the first place. Some may have low faith. They want to pursue the goal, but are easily shaken by adversity. Others may initially put forth a good effort, but their persistence gradually erodes. Often they surrender when success is imminent. They run out of breath on the 99th yard of the 100-yard dash.

Persistence Can Erode

The Power of Persistence is something we can unconsciously erode on a daily basis when we don't follow through on the things we say we intend to do. This behavior can become the seed of a quitter's mentality and ingrain procrastination into our personality while displacing a mentality of committed action.

Lack of courage also undermines persistence in the face of challenges. As courage is the antidote to fear, lack of courage is an indicator that some type of fear has overwhelmed you. When you are not able to override the paralysis that the fear you feel generates, your ability to decide and act is destroyed. Very often, boosting your sense of confidence and competence through preparation, practice, and solid planning will help override fear. Any remaining gap in confidence may be closed by a strong sense of faith that allows you to deal with circumstances beyond your control. Stretching your limits with new endeavors that push you out of your comfort zone can be very effective in strengthening your Power of Persistence. This exercise provides proof that you can endure greater challenges and succeed.

Criticism

Criticism is a common roadblock to your Power of Persistence. We can never control what others will say. It seems that the chorus of naysayers starts to sing just as you begin to pour your energy into your pursuits. The chorus seems to instinctively know to reach crescendo just as you near the attainment of your goals. Benjamin Franklin clearly expressed his views regarding people who are prone to criticizing:

"Any fool can criticize, condemn, and complain and most fools do."

Largely, the chorus of naysayers is composed of people who have no courage to take risks in pursuit of anything. Such people can never see what's possible and only focus on the difficult. The only way the naysayers can feel better about their own reticence is to amass as much company as possible in the naysayer chorus.

Sadly, the first members in the naysayer chorus are often our parents. Overcritical parents are often driven by a fear of seeing their children hurt. It's a form of misguided love. Sometimes, however, our parents' criticism is driven by repressed regret over not pursuing their own dreams, and their criticism is a reflexive reaction to their unconscious inner need for superiority over their children. The impact can be devastating on the developing psyche of a child. Fortunately, you know that through introspection and by evoking your Power of Poise, any latent fear of criticism can be overcome. You are the owner of your emotions, regardless of how your dominant, recurring emotions originated. As the owner, you can discard useless emotions whenever you choose.

If you find yourself being criticized for reasons you don't quite understand, the criticism may be driven by envy. Take this as an odd compliment. Dale Carnegie expressed this perspective when he quipped:

"No one ever kicks a dead dog."

Therefore, if you are drawing criticism, your idea or endeavor may actually have real value that makes some people feel threatened. By drawing on your Power of Poise, you will begin to realize that you shouldn't have any part of your self-worth vested in what anyone else thinks.

Last, understanding the value of some types of criticism is important. Automatically dismissing valid criticism can be as detrimental to a leader as scrapping an idea because of invalid criticism. Sometimes people are truly trying to be objective. They may raise a good point without expressing it well. Their words may antagonize, and the value of their message is lost. Your ability to listen effectively will help you accept constructive criticism.

4 Power Thoughts

1. Does criticism overwhelm you when you set out in pursuit of a goal?
   a. Think of ways to increase your competence as a way of boosting your courage and confidence.
2. Do you find yourself making excuses at the first sign of difficulty?
   a. Examine your commitment to your goals and the value of those goals in your life.

CHAPTER 35

Persistence Achieved

"If not today, another way. If not that way, another day."

– Dan Shyti

N o goal worth pursuing is ever easy. By keeping this thought in the forefront of your mind, you can prepare yourself for any resistance you encounter. You can conquer the fear of failure by realizing that, since you are in control of how many times you get to try, failure does not occur until you quit.

Develop a habit of following through on your daily agenda. Whatever you said you would do on your "To Do" list, do it! Get into the habit of completing tasks. Start small and work toward bigger goals.

Achieving the Power of Persistence means that when confronted with a challenge, you are a leader who starts with "yes" and immediately focuses on "how." You are not immobilized by fear. You engage your virtue of courage to override fear and give you strength to stick to your principles when confronted with a moral dilemma. You do not let criticism prevent you from pursuing your goals. As a leader who has developed a thick skin, you let criticism roll off your back. You never surrender.

Having covered the Power of Persistence, you have now learned the entire 4 Power Leadership Framework and the philosophy behind it. You can now use the framework in your daily life to gauge your leadership effectiveness.

Poise   Self-possession and full self-knowledge.

- Did I live in accordance with virtue today?
- Am I maintaining a calm inner core that is virtue-focused?
- Do I feel confident?
- Am I in full possession and control of my emotions?

Presence   The ability to project our confident inner self as a means of radiating confidence to others.

- Does my inner confidence and high self-esteem shine outwardly?
- Am I projecting a leadership image that inspires confidence and respect?

Performance The core ability to generate results.

- Have I received the necessary feedback to ensure that plans are on track?
- Am I maintaining a focus on attaining desired results in all that I do as a leader?
- Do I empower and hold others accountable?
- Do I seek continuous improvement in skills and knowledge required by my job?

Persistence The fuel for achievement that enables you to push past all resistance encountered in the pursuit of goals.

- Am I tenacious in the face of adversity?
- Am I undaunted by obstacles I encounter?
- Did I vacillate in any decisions or courses of action?
- Am I committed to my team's current direction?

4 Power Thoughts

1. Persistence depends on developing and maintaining habits that enhance your leadership qualities.
   a. What bad habits do you have that may undermine your Power of Persistence?
2. Develop a daily habit of assessing your leadership performance based on the 4 Power Leadership Framework.

Section 5
The Things that Matter Most

CHAPTER 36

Cast a Good Shadow

"Character is like a tree and reputation like a shadow. The shadow is what we think of it; the tree is the real thing."

– Abraham Lincoln

L eaders are role models. There is no escaping that responsibility. People will look to you to set an example, and your example is communicated most broadly by your reputation. Reputation is what people say and think about you when you're not present. It arrives on the scene long before you do. Reputation determines whether you receive a choice assignment from your company. With customers, it determines whether you or your competitors are awarded a multimillion-dollar contract. Most importantly, reputation is what your subordinates check on long before they accept you as their leader.

All It Takes Is One Bad Decision

A reputation can take a lifetime to build and only moments to severely damage or even completely destroy. The damage can occur through a single moment of bad judgment, one misdeed, or as a culmination of deep and recurring character flaws. There's a frailty to human character that can unexpectedly emerge when we are presented with a delicate choice. Some people are quick and consistent in engaging their virtues and choose the right course while others leave you wondering what in the world they were thinking. Since we are all potentially vulnerable to human fallibility, we must be constantly vigilant in avoiding the blunders that take down otherwise illustrious careers. The scandal hungry media ultimately discovers, amplifies, and rebroadcasts the misdeeds of prominent people. Once publicized, there's no escape from the onslaught of negative public sentiment that follows.

The wall of shame that illustrates how easily reputations can be ruined is broad indeed. In November 2012, Christopher Kubasik, CEO-elect of defense contractor Lockheed-Martin, was forced to resign after an inappropriate relationship with a subordinate employee came to light.[9] Imagine the bitterness he generated for himself in losing the crowning assignment of his career due to his own poor judgment.

In another similar incident, Kenneth Melani, former CEO of health insurance company, Highmark was forced to resign in April 2012 due to an affair and the subsequent lies he told to the board of directors about the affair.[10] The incident nearly destroyed his entire life. His lover's husband pummeled him and many of his friends abandoned him due to his indiscretion.

Also in April 2012, Brian Dunn, former CEO of Best Buy, was forced to resign because a company investigation revealed that he had an affair with a female employee.[11] Dunn had started his storied carrier at Best Buy as a sales clerk and rose all the way to the top post. When Dunn's career crashed rather abruptly, he took

---

[9] "Lockheed-Martin CEO-Elect Kubasik Fired Over Improper Relationship With Female Subordinate," Agustino Fontevecchia, Forbes Online, November 9, 2012

[10] "Fired Highmark CEO says affair backlash was 'catastrophic'," Associated Press, June 08, 2012.

[11] Also, "Lockheed-Martin CEO-Elect Kubasik Fired Over Improper Relationship With Female Subordinate," Agustino Fontevecchia, Forbes Online, November 9, 2012

the reputation of company founder Robert Schulze down with him. Schulze made the added poor choice of trying to help cover Dunn's affair. This is another example of a leader compounding a bad situation, as I mentioned earlier, by engaging in a cover-up instead of full disclosure.

Then we have the cheating scandals in professional sports such as steroids in baseball and doping in cycling, with the most shocking situation of all being the extraordinary obliteration of Lance Armstrong's reputation. His repeated, systematic, and almost pathological denials put him in a category all his own.

Can a reputation be recovered after a misdeed comes to light? The answer really depends on the circumstances and severity of the misdeed and the power of the platform that the discredited public figure can leverage to rehabilitate his image. One thing is for sure: the probability of recovery is severely diminished if the public figure chooses denial of a factual allegation as his defense. When proof does come to light, the public figure takes two hits – one for bad judgment and another for dishonesty. Instead, if the public figure is indeed guilty of the alleged misdeed, the sooner he comes clean and makes an earnest apology, the higher his chances are for recovery. Again, depending on circumstances, the public is at times willing to forgive.

Be a Model Citizen

No matter what profession you're in, a solid reputation has always been important in the business arena. In today's hypermedia age, reputations are particularly fragile. When a politician or any other public figure is involved in a scandal, the Internet makes it possible for even someone in the most remote corner of the earth to learn about it instantly. Regardless of your leadership level, build your reputation methodically based on a sterling character.

Then, guard that reputation fiercely by adherence to virtue, sound principles, and a keen eye for unscrupulous people who will try to sully your reputation unjustly.

Reputation is central to your identity and authority. You must proactively maintain and enhance it. Start by maintaining appropriate online behavior. You must operate under the assumption that everything you do or post online will be retrievable indefinitely and one day will come to light when you least expect it.

Secondly, your public demeanor must always support your image as someone who should be taken seriously. The image of a leader is incompatible with self-degrading buffoonery, drunkenness, or any other behavioral aberration that undercuts the Power of Presence. You should only engage in humor in limited doses to display a sharp wit as a means of enhancing your presence. The occasional well-timed, self-deprecating remark is also useful in demonstrating that, while you expect to be taken seriously, you are also secure enough in your own self-image to laugh at yourself.

Avoid vulgarity and don't engage in any behavior that detracts from your image as an outstanding citizen. You should set your own high standard of conduct for yourself and not accept the low bar that society sets for the average person. Despite living in what superficially seems as a socially liberal era, people are always ready to look down their noses at someone who engages in loose conduct of any kind. People always expect their leaders to rise above the common social behavioral norm. Therefore, your conduct must serve the explicit purpose of building your reputation as a solid model citizen and avoiding even the appearance of impropriety.

One of the best ways to be a model citizen and simultaneously enhance your image as trustworthy and loyal is to defend the reputation of others when they are maligned in their absence.

Have you ever been present when a group of people begins to attack someone who is not present? Build a reputation for loyalty and honesty by simply saying you would rather discuss any issues with the person in question when he or she is present. Respect for you will rise in the eyes of those who observe that you are not the type that engages in backstabbing. Further, for those who do engage in backstabbing, how do you think others will look upon them? If someone approaches you and begins to malign a colleague, you can bet one day they will do it to you too. Boost your reputation by refusing to participate in maligning others.

Lincoln was an astute observer of character, and he made sure that he always kept his own character strong. His analogy of the tree and shadow is so fitting when examining character and reputation. Shadows are cast when an object blocks light. Interestingly, shadows are cast in an elongated and distorted fashion. Sometimes, shadows are seen before you actually see the object that created them. In turn, the light reflected by the object is what allows you to see the actual object. It's your task to make sure that your character is seen in the best possible light. Your character must also have substance to cast a good shadow and for people to see your character well. If your character (the tree) is thin, your reputation (the shadow) will be poor.

Dependability Enhances Presence

Rising to a challenge and leading important company initiatives will further enhance your reputation as a dependable leader. Sometimes, special initiatives can be high risk because companies occasionally choose to operate outside their comfort zone in pursuit of growth opportunities. Carefully choose initiatives to lead that have realistic and achievable goals. I've personally experienced both success and failure with regard to leading important initiatives, but in both cases my reputation was enhanced.

In an example of success, I inherited a business development department that was in disarray and was internally maligned for lack of consistent success. The persons responsible for the poor performance had left, and the team that remained needed to be refocused and reenergized. Fortunately, I was able to turn this team around and the team achieved great success during my tenure. The lion's share of the credit belongs to my team members, because they embraced their functions, accepted ownership of critical actions, and executed skillfully. However, I also credit this success to the application of sound leadership principles, and of course, some fortuitous timing.

In a subsequent assignment, things didn't go as well. My company hastily partnered with a software company whose core product was extremely innovative and addressed the needs of an emerging market space. The claimed capabilities of the software were never fully verified prior to my company signing a joint marketing deal. Later on, we suffered from repeated project setbacks as snags were encountered. Looking back, my company was overreaching by entering a line of business in which we had no experience. By the time I took over leadership of the initiative, the situation unraveled faster than I could fix it. A series of poor decisions made before I assumed control set me up for failure and the situation was not retrievable.

Through this experience, I learned a valuable lesson in the importance of following my intuition. Prior to accepting the assignment, I had told my division president that I wanted to test the software before I committed to the job. I later changed my mind and chose to accept the assignment anyway without first verifying the software's capability. My original instinct to trust-but-verify was the right decision in retrospect. Had I done so, I could have avoided having my name attached to a failed project. Fortunately, I did score some points with my division president, who appreciated my stepping up for this assignment. However, I've since committed to paying more attention to my gut instincts.

I have advanced my career numerous times by developing a reputation for taking on tough assignments willingly. Tough assignments can be career makers that enhance your reputation as long as they are mission possible. However, even if you take a chance on a challenging assignment and come up short, your reputation as someone who is willing to take on a challenge can still work in your favor.

Truth in Advertising

If you are of good character and you want a good reputation, not only must you act properly, but those around you must also be made aware of your solid ability and accomplishments. This is not easy for a virtuous leader, because advertising your accomplishments goes against the virtue of humility. You should practice the skill of promoting your accomplishments without sounding boastful. You must also be careful to give credit to your team. Remember that as a leader, you earn your money by organizing others, not by doing all the work yourself. Leaders who claim all the credit for their team's accomplishments wind up appearing small and insecure instead of powerful and capable.

4 Power Thoughts

1. Assess your reputation.
   a. What would you change?
2. What labels are most commonly used to describe you?
   a. What are the pros and cons of these labels?
3. Have you ever witnessed a situation in your company where someone injured his reputation?
   a. What went wrong and why?
   b. Were they able to recover their reputation?

CHAPTER 37

Your Call to Action

"Some men must follow, and some command, though all are made of clay."

– Henry Wadsworth Longfellow

Y ou have now read a great deal on an important subject, but there's always more to learn that you can apply in your daily life as a leader. An old friend of mine once described an expert as a person incapable of further learning. I have also heard that an expert is someone who has made every mistake at least once. Whenever I hear the word "expert," I can't help but think of these humorous definitions. Humor aside, being an expert really means you've dedicated yourself to a level of learning that distinguishes you among your peers. Just don't become someone who thinks he knows it all, because then you just might fit my friend's definition.

Leaders who stop learning set themselves up for failure. You must always be ready and willing to apply new methods and approaches to maintain the welfare and peak performance of the organization you lead.

Tap the Fountains of Knowledge

The more we do and experience, the more we form indelible lessons from which we can draw strength to make future decisions. However, learning through experience is severely constrained, because we cannot accumulate personal experience any faster than time and circumstances allow. That's why learning from others is pivotal in accumulating a wealth of experience faster than simply living our own lives. Sometimes our experience is derived from encountering failure. While we always want to avert failure, deriving valuable lessons from our mistakes is a powerful source of learning. Oscar Wilde, author, poet, and playwright noted:

"Experience is simply the name we give our mistakes."

However, there is absolutely no requirement to repeat the mistakes that others have already made as a way to achieve personal competence. This concept is the greatest tool that you have for closing any experience gap and saving enormous amounts of time. As Eleanor Roosevelt wisely said:

"Learn from the mistakes of others. You can't live long enough to make them all yourself."

Further, anytime you are exposed to people who have experience in a given area that interests you, it's an opportunity to converse with them on the subject. Constantly seek out opportunities to associate with people smarter and more experienced than yourself. You will be amazed at how fast their positive qualities and ideas can be absorbed and emulated. When properly approached with a considerate attitude, most people will gladly share their experience and knowledge.

This concept also applies to people far below you on the organizational ladder. Don't ever let your ego dismiss these valuable frontline employees. Ask probing questions and solicit their opinions often. The feedback you receive will include information about situations, approaches to problem resolution, and outcomes of past approaches. Most importantly, you'll gain insight into the range of emotions displayed by the people involved. You know that leadership is a people business, so the emotional component of learning should never be neglected.

As I have already noted, the largest pool of knowledge available to you is experience based on the lives of historic people. Therefore, become a committed reader. You can reach across the experience base of vast segments of human history just by reading. Great leaders have themselves employed this program of learning. For example, Charles de Gaulle once quipped:

> "Don't ask me who's influenced me. A lion is made up of the lambs he's digested, and I've been reading all my life."

Lincoln and Churchill were both avid readers. Churchill even won a Pulitzer Prize for writing. Many of the Founding Fathers maintained extensive libraries at a time when a book cost more than a month's salary for the average worker. *Reading expands a leader's horizons and ability to formulate a vision like no other tool.*

Perspective

Our lives are a speck when compared to the vastness of the universe where time is measured relative to the speed of light. When we observe distant stars, we are not really observing the physical objects as they exist today, but the light that left those objects years before. If we were to attempt to travel to those stars, it would take thousands of years to get there, and by the time we arrive, the objects we observed from earth may no longer exist. Why should we consume any time at all thinking about all this? The answer is simple – perspective.

When I think of the wonders of the universe, I stand in awe of God's creation. I stay grounded this way. I know that when I have achieved success, it is fleeting. Conversely, when times are bad, I take heart that my troubles too will soon pass. Once you have a true sense of scale and perspective of where you fit in the grand scheme of things, I hope you can refocus your thoughts on what truly matters in life.

No matter how great we become as leaders; no matter how many buildings we build; no matter how many wars we win; no matter how many billions of dollars we amass; no matter how many championships we hang on our walls – the sun will rise and set tomorrow, and those distant stars will still shine forth from yesterday. Even the most powerful leaders have to face that one last task that cannot be delegated. That last task is the great equalizer. Take heart and don't look at such a heavy thought as depressing, but rather as a valuable dose of humility, which is the antidote to a leader's worst enemy – hubris.

Hubris is a leader's worst enemy because it originates in one's own heart and can slowly displace all virtues if not restrained. If you feel hubris creeping into your heart, consider this:

"If you are humble, nothing will touch you, neither praise nor disgrace because you know what you are. If you are blamed, you won't be discouraged; if anyone calls you a saint, you won't put yourself on a pedestal."

- Mother Teresa

Choose Your Legacy

What kind of world could we have if leaders focused on what matters most – positively impacting the lives of other people, setting an example of virtue, and sparing as much pain as possible?

If you were in your last moment of life, what kind of legacy would you want to leave behind? Wouldn't you want to be able to look back on a legacy of leadership where you can say, "I made the world a better place for as many people as I could?"

Leading in harmony with virtues can provide a lifetime of fulfillment because it requires you to be at your best. When we lead in this way, we are living up to who we were meant to be.

In closing, no matter the heights you reach, always maintain the human touch. Never lose your ability to connect with others on an individual level. This assures that your journey in leadership will always remain fulfilling, despite the challenges along the way.

> *"Every day you may make progress. Every step may be fruitful. Yet there will stretch out before you an ever-lengthening, ever-ascending, ever-improving path. You know you will never get to the end of the journey. But this, so far from discouraging, only adds to the joy and glory of the climb."*
>
> *– Sir Winston Churchill*

It's now time for you to act. Enjoy your climb as a 4 Power Leader.

Final 4 Power Thought

What is the first improvement you will make to your leadership approach starting immediately? Take action and improve continuously.

References

1) Aristotle, and J. A. K. Thomson. *The Ethics Aristotle: The Nicomachean Ethics.* Harmondsworth, etc.: Penguin, 1976. Print.

2) Brodie, Fawn McKay. *Thomas Jefferson, an Intimate History.* New York: Norton, 1974. Print.

3) Brookhiser, Richard. *James Madison.* New York, NY: Basic, 2011. Print.

4) Carnegie, Dale. *Dale Carnegie's Lifetime Plan for Success: How to Win Friends & Influence People; How to Stop Worrying & Start Living: The Great Bestselling Works Complete in One Volume.* New York: Galahad, 1998. Print.

5) Covey, Stephen R *Principle-Centered Leadership.* New York: Summit, 1991. Print.

6) Franklin, Benjamin. *The Autobiography of Benjamin Franklin.* New York: Barnes & Noble, 2005. Print.

7) Gaffney, Steven. *Honesty Works!* Arlington, VA: JMG, 2006. Print.

8) Gandhi, Mohandas Karamchand, Mahadev Haribhai Desai, and Sissela Bok. *An Autobiography.* Boston: Beacon, 1993. Print.

9) Gracián, Y. Morales, Baltasar, Martin Fischer, and Steven Schroeder. *The Art of Worldly Wisdom.* New York: Barnes & Noble, 2008. Print.

10) Greene, Robert, and Joost Elffers. *The 48 Laws of Power.* New York: Penguin, 2000. Print.

11) Herold, J. Christopher. *The Age of Napoleon.* New York: American Heritage, 1985. Print.

12) Hill, Napoleon. *Think and Grow Rich.* Greenwich, CT: Fawcett Crest, 1960. Print.

13) Humes, James C. *Speak like Churchill, Stand like Lincoln: 21 Powerful Secrets of History's Greatest Speakers.* New York: Three Rivers, 2002. Print.

14) Irving, Washington, and Charles Neider. *George Washington: A Biography*: Illustrated. New York: Da Capo, 1994. Print.

15) Isaacson, Walter. *Benjamin Franklin: An American Life.* New York: Simon & Schuster, 2003. Print.

16) Jefferson, Thomas, and John P. Kaminski. *The Quotable Jefferson.* Princeton, NJ: Princeton UP, 2006. Print.

17) Kouzes, James M., and Barry Z. Posner. *The Leadership Challenge.* San Francisco, CA: Jossey-Bass, 2007. Print.

18) Lincoln, Abraham, and John Gabriel Hunt. *The Essential Abraham Lincoln.* New York: Gramercy, 1993. Print.

19) Lombardi, Vince. *The Lombardi Rules: 26 Lessons from Vince Lombardi – the World's Greatest Coach.* New York: McGraw-Hill, 2003. Print.

20) Lombardi, Vince. *What It Takes to Be #1: Vince Lombardi on Leadership.* New York: McGraw-Hill, 2001. Print.

21) Lovell, Jim, and Jeffrey Kluger. *Lost Moon: The Perilous Voyage of Apollo 13.* Boston: Houghton Mifflin, 1994. Print.

22) McCullough, David G. *John Adams.* New York: Simon & Schuster, 2001. Print.

23) Meier, Christian. *Caesar: A Biography.* New York: Basic, 1982. Print.

24) O'Connor, Joseph, John Seymour, Robert Dilts, and John Grinder. *Introducing NLP: Psychological Skills for Understanding and Influencing People.* San Francisco, CA: Conari, 2011. Print.

25) Phillips, Donald T. *Lincoln on Leadership: Executive Strategies for Tough times.* New York: Warner, 1993. Print.

26) Plato, and G. M. A. Grube. *Five Dialogues.* Indianapolis, IN: Hackett Pub., 2002. Print.

27) Potter, D. S. *Emperors of Rome: The Story of Imperial Rome from Julius Caesar to the Last Emperor.* London: Quercus, 2007. Print.

28) Robbins, Anthony. *Awaken the Giant Within: How to Take Immediate Control of Your Mental, Emotional, Physical & Financial Destiny.* New York, NY: Summit, 1991. Print.

29) Robbins, Anthony. *Unlimited Power.* London: Simon & Schuster, 1998. Print.

30) Shafritz, Jay M., and J. Steven. Ott. *Classics of Organization Theory.* Pacific Grove, CA: Brooks/Cole Pub., 1992. Print.

31) Shapiro, Fred R. *The Yale Book of Quotations.* New Haven: Yale UP, 2006. Print.

32) Slater, Robert, and Jack Welch. *Jack Welch on Leadership: Abridged from Jack Welch and the GE Way.* New York: McGraw-Hill, 2004. Print.

33) Teresa, and Carol Kelly-Gangi. *Mother Teresa, Her Essential Wisdom.* New York: Barnes & Noble, 2006. Print.

34) Thatcher, Margaret. *The Path to Power.* New York: Harper Collins, 1995. Print.

35) Thomas, Benjamin Platt. *Abraham Lincoln: A Biography.* New York: Barnes & Noble, 1993. Print.

Index

ABOUT THE AUTHOR

Daniel A. (Dan) Shyti is an author, speaker, and mentor specializing in leadership training. He is the founder of 4 Power Leadership, a company dedicated to leadership training for corporate and government clients. Services include leadership seminars, keynote speaking, executive coaching, and public speaking training.

Dan is formerly a Vice President at L-3, a major technology and defense company. He has held various leadership positions in corporations and the military for 26 years of his 30-year career. Dan delivers practical and effective leadership training by drawing from his experience and his years of research in isolating the key characteristics that great leaders possess.

Dan is a graduate of Pratt Institute, where he earned a Bachelor of Science Degree in Electrical Engineering. He is also a distinguished military graduate of the Brooklyn Polytechnic University's Reserve Officer Training Corps (ROTC) program. Dan served four years with distinction in the Army attaining the rank of Captain.

Seminar Information

For Information about upcoming 4 Power Leadership seminars, visit www.4PowerLeadership.com or send an email to inquiry@4PowerLeadership.com.

www.ingramcontent.com/pod-product-compliance
Lightning Source LLC
Chambersburg PA
CBHW060005100426

42740CB00010B/1402